TRANSFORMED BY GOD'S GRACE

Transformed by God's Grace

Dr. Jessica and Pastor David Swain

XULON PRESS

Xulon Press
2301 Lucien Way #415
Maitland, FL 32751
407.339.4217
www.xulonpress.com

Paperback ISBN-13: 978-1-66284-659-5

DEDICATION

1 Corinthians 13:4–7 (NIV)—Love is patient, love is kind. It does not envy, it does not boast, it is not proud. It does not dishonor others, it is not self-seeking, it is not easily angered, it keeps no record of wrongs. Love does not delight in evil but rejoices with the truth. It always protects, always trusts, always hopes, always perseveres.

To my husband David, who has become a man of integrity, honor, and wisdom. Thank you for your love and never-ending devotion. Thank you for being the man God called you to be and going through God's transforming grace with me.

To my children, Kris and JaBaris, thank you for your love and dedication of not so perfect parents. You brought out and represent the best part of our love.

TABLE OF CONTENTS

FOREWORD

IT HAS BEEN a great privilege to know Dr. Jessica and David Swain for more than 25 years. Dr. Swain is an educator, instructor, marriage enrichment counselor, and a minister of God's Word. Her ministry and teachings come from a deep passion to help families, particularly married couples, and a commitment to God and His Word. Dr. Swain has a profound experience of walking with the Lord Jesus. This experience has been weaved into the writing of *Transformed by God's Grace*.

Transformed by God's Grace is more than another good manual on marriage. It is, instead, a powerful tool that will help every person who desires to get married, married couples who desire to experience more fulfillment in marriage, and finally, those whose marriage may need a tune-up. Though written as a personal testimony, this book answers many of the questions that couples ask during marriage counseling. It addresses issues that many couples confront in marriage and things people can do to strengthen their marriage relationship.

One thing I particularly like about ***Transformed by God's Grace*** is that it is easy to read. Though it includes theological concepts, this is not a theological book. When I picked up the manuscript of this book to read, I could not stop reading until I came to the last page. As a pastor, author, and minister of God's Word and marriage counselor, I believe this is a must-read book. I am looking forward to purchasing copies of this book to share with friends.

Pastor N. George Utuk, Ph.D.
Founder and Pastor
Abundant Life Word Fellowship

I've known Jessica for many years as a friend, professional, and ministry leader. She demonstrates professional candor as a person, former school principal, and church leader. Her intentional and purposeful submission that transformed her life and marriage guided her to pen the book ***Transformed by God's Grace***. It is a compass to help others avoid marriage pitfalls, as well as a roadmap for singles to prepare for marriage.

This book presents insightful adventures that led to Kairos outcomes. The book gives wisdom from her life and marriage experiences commenced as emotional turbulence but continues with guided landings. This book takes you on a journey through plot twists to help develop and grow your marriage in God's way with a willing heart to submit to the plan He has, rather than a self-aggrandized agenda.

Proverbs 16:9 says, "A man's heart plans his way, But the LORD directs his steps." This book shares how men can plan their way, but it is God who directs their steps juxtaposed by spiritual principles for maximum impact unashamedly doing it God's way for the benefit and development of life and marriage.

Let this book take you from a potential divorce statistic halted by "detours that interrupt the journey to where God had to change your mind to blow your mind."

Debra Causey, Minister

I not only read this book, ***Transformed by God's Grace***, but I am extremely proud to add my voice of appreciation to this timely and priceless work of grace that explodes on every page in the lives of David and Jessica Swain.

Through their journey of God's redemptive work in their marriage, you can see the wording and preparation of God's hand for their present ministry assignment that involves equipping and empowering married couples to develop a Christ-centered relationship through In His Will Marriage Ministry. We are very honored to have them as our spiritual children and family.

This book is a must reading for everyone who is willing to invite God's grace into their lives to transform their relationships and marriages.

Pastor Arthur Wade
Pastor and Founder
New Anointing Family Worship Center
Jacksonville, Florida

This book, ***Transformed by God's Grace***, has taught me something that the Bible says we should do when it comes to submission. In my mind, I too, thought it meant to be controlled and I have been there. Now, I see that submission means having an attitude and lifestyle of serving one another. I have witnessed submission in the lives of David and Jessica, and I know this marriage alone has pleased God. To the readers of this book, I say that you will learn so many things you were not taught, but I also say it's better late than never and to see how we can be misled by the enemy, the flesh, and other people.

The Swains have been very transparent, which is what we all need because, in doing so, there are many people who will be helped by reading, trusting, and learning things from this book that many of us have gone through but were fearful to say. Believe me, the information in this book will set you free.

Co-Pastor Pauline Wade,
Co-Pastor and Founder
New Anointing Family Worship Center
Jacksonville, Florida

Chapter One

How Our Story Began

"What therefore God hath joined
together, let not man put asunder."
— Mark 10:9 (KJV)

A WEDDING IS one of the biggest and most involved events you may ever bring together. You may have been in a wedding or two, or maybe one of your close friends recently got married. Unfortunately, things are a lot different when it is your wedding. You may have also found out you had NO idea where to start. You probably dove headfirst into budgets and guest lists and made your way through all the other steps that were essential to make your wedding the event of a lifetime. There is a heightened sense of excitement knowing that you have finally met the love of your life and you will live happily ever after. You start visualizing all the wonderful times you will have and how each day will be nothing but love. In fact, you can't imagine it being any other way. At least, that is what you start out believing.

It is simply amazing how we spend so much time laying out our plans for marriage. We hire a wedding consultant or an event planner or better yet, we use the skills, knowledge, and ability of our best friend. Your best friend probably never planned a wedding before, and she thought this event was her breakout moment. Oh, and before I go on, let me say, that having your best friend plan your wedding is probably not the best idea. Even the best of friends can fall out over the smallest things during wedding planning. Even so, we spend a lot of time in the details of selecting colors, picking out dresses and tuxedos, selecting a menu for the grand occasion, deciding on who will be in the wedding, who will get to attend the wedding, where will we hold the wedding, and who will oversee the ceremony. Each detail becomes more and more complex as we navigate through the maze of planning. Let's not forgot how the soon to be in-laws will fit into the wedding plans. You know, things like how the mother-in-law dreamed of her son's wedding being an epic event that centered around the groom and his family. You probably didn't realize that your mother planned to make your wedding, the wedding she never had. Perhaps amid the love whirlwind, you weren't paying attention to family backgrounds or religious affiliations. Differing religious preferences among family members can cause all kinds of conflict and disagreement. Traditional religious views about the wedding ceremony can bump heads with more modern views about weddings. The simplest wedding can become extremely complicated just trying to make everyone happy. Unfortunately, our planning and expectations for the wedding can leave out the most important wedding planner, God.

You see, God is the greatest wedding planner for an event of this magnitude. We tend to leave Him out of our planning, and in most cases, we don't take the time to consider that God needs to be involved in even the tiniest details. Sadly, many couples don't know God when they get married. The wedding is the jump off celebration to get the marriage started. Who better than the Holy Spirit to set off the warning lights when a train is on the same track that you are on? I am going to state for the record that we need God to be in on every detail. At best, we tend to take a moment to do a quick consult with God right before we say those two famous words, I do. Those words seem so warm and fuzzy when we hear them uttered by the one person, we believe we will spend the rest of our lives with. We swirl at the anticipation of life ahead, especially the night ahead, and then the magical kiss that closes the deal for most of us.

Now, let us not leave out the honeymoon. It is the consummation event we have been waiting for unless we have already done a test drive. We spend our days in marital bliss anxiously anticipating the days and years ahead. Each one of us has decided what this new union will look like and how we will forge ahead. We didn't take the time before the marriage to address some of the most important topics in a marriage. You know, things like, where will we live? Will we have children? How many children do we want to have? Will your mother be calling us every day? Do we have credit card debt? Have either of us been married before? What church will we attend? Do either of us go to a church? Do we believe in God? These questions can go on and on, and it is interesting to note that many couples never sit down to ask these questions before they get married. It's almost as if, the "don't ask don't tell" policy applies. We rely on a marriage counselor, or a pastor to give us the quick version of meeting the state requirements for marriage, but we never spend the time to get to the deep stuff that can be a little challenging. I've found that some pastors (no disrespect), have reckless lives themselves and are not equipped to provide marriage enrichment, counseling, preparation, or anything remotely like giving marital advice. There are those of us who never received marriage counseling or marriage enrichment. We jumped right into the marriage with both feet, excited about each other and the future ahead. We didn't know or realize that one day we would ask ourselves "What were we thinking?" Why were we in such a hurry? Were there events that created such a rush for us to get married and we took the jump and thought about it later? Well, David and I were in the group of those who jumped first and then thought about it later. Circumstances and situations catapulted us into making decisions that launched us in a direction that we never intended. We were under pressure and the decisions we made had long-term repercussions.

David and I both came from very dysfunctional homes. We were children of parents who did not have an ounce of knowledge of what a real marriage looked like, let alone what a positive relationship looked like. They also did not know Jesus Christ. The only thing my parents knew was that you got married and you fought it out until you could not stand it anymore. If all else fails, you just walk away. You could bail just like you bail from an airplane—quick and in a hurry. That seemed to be the more convenient approach during those days. The only problem with that idea is that couples fail to realize if children are involved, it is not a quick drop and roll. The damage is deep. It goes through you and on to your children, who may spend much of their lives wondering if there was something they could have done to help mommy and daddy stay married. Children may entertain the idea that if they had behaved better, mommy and daddy would still be married. They may begin to secretly harbor resentment because they may not understand what was so hard to overcome in the marriage. They may even feel that their lives have been destroyed because of the decisions their parents made. David and I hadn't surveyed the damage to ourselves, so we didn't realize how encumbered we were with issues from our relationship. In many cases, couples who end up divorced take the same dysfunctional behavior of the first marriage to their next marriage.

I was a child of what I like to describe as "tug of war" parents. I was a young child caught in the middle of a war of wills between two dysfunctional people. It was a war that my mother, unfortunately, lost to my father. Neither of my parents were any better nor would they be considered parents of the year. They were both alcoholics, and they both fought demons from their pasts. David, on the other hand, was raised by his aunts and his grandparents. He was one of four children. His mother resided in Atlanta, Georgia where she raised his younger brothers and sister. David was left with his aunt and grandparents in Eatonton, Georgia. His father was never married to his mother. Sometime during David's teen years, his father shot and killed his wife and then killed himself. What a legacy to leave your son? To be remembered as the son of a man who killed his wife and then killed himself. It is simply ironic how parents fail to realize, the things their children see them do, and experience, will frame the narrative of their children's adult lives. Our parents didn't understand the damage they had done.

When we graduated from high school, we felt the wind push us to each other and into a future of uncertainty. My father and grandmother died a month apart, which were only a few days after my high school graduation. I was a high school graduate; immediately left alone by the two people I cherished the most. I had to plan two funerals essentially right after I flipped my graduation tassel. I was fortunate to be surrounded by people who helped me plan the funerals and take care of all the necessary details that came with funeral planning. I remember contacting my mother to notify her of my father's death. Now, notifying my mother is where I began to see the seeds of hurt and despair on display by a wounded person. My mother came to my father's funeral wearing a red dress. Talk about the devil wears Prada. When I think back on this, I laugh at the looks and gasps of the mothers of the church when my mother stepped in there with that red dress on. I guess in her own way, she was telling my father that she had the last laugh. As hurtful and disappointing as it was to me, it was a true line in the sand of how marital hurt can be so deep. I will say that my mother probably never realized that she hammered a huge nail in her own coffin when it came to me. How dare she disrespect my father. I learned then that hurt people hurt other people, even if it means they must disrespect them in death. I guess my mother couldn't deal with my father in life, so she took that opportunity to deal with him in death. My mother's red dress was a symbol of how determined she was to declare her independence from my father. He was dead and she was alive to declare victory. What a sad commentary of the type of life she led and would continue to lead. My mother was bitter and resentful, and she generously passed those feelings on to me.

Regardless of the situations and circumstances that had come to pass, David and I did not have any thoughts about how our lives should be or what we should do. We thought we were free from the shackles of dysfunction and on our way to what we considered a better life. We were going to be together, and we were going to do it our way. We were going to show everyone in our families that just because our parents were a mess, it didn't mean we were going to be a mess. Spoiler alert: We were truly misguided with that thinking.

Oh, did I mention that both of us grew up in the church? Perhaps, I should say that both of us attended church when we were young. David and I both had wonderful grandparents who always believed that we must go to a church no matter what happened. God would help us and take care of us. Above all, they believed in the scripture in Proverbs 22:6 (KJV), which states, "Train up a child in the way he should go: and when he is old, he will not depart from it." I am sure now that they both believed that no matter where life took us, we would not fall away from God. At least, if we slid down the slippery slope of life, God would eventually get us back on track. It is a true statement when I say somebody prayed for us. In fact, I am convinced that in our darkest hours, we rode on some of those old prayers. Even when we did not know God, He knew us. I still believe, even until this day, we are still riding on our grandmamma's prayers.

Now, this is where I tell you that after all these wonderful wedding descriptions, I now must tell you that we didn't quite have that kind of wedding. We had a wedding, but it was more like a 30-minute car wash. We ran through the wash cycle, hit the most important parts, and drove away. David and I didn't get the joy and privilege of planning a great wedding and all the excitement that I described. I believe my daughter had that wedding. Instead, what we had was a quick, down and dirty marriage after church services. We lived together for about a month unmarried and we were haunted by the thoughts of the sin we were committing. It was like living under an enormous cloud that reminded us each day, that what we were doing was wrong. I am not exaggerating when I say that we could hear our grandparents telling us that we knew better than to be living in sin. Eventually, it was too overwhelming, and we surrendered to the idea of getting married. As I think back, getting married just seemed to be better than living in sin. So, we came home from Atlanta, Georgia, one weekend and told David's Aunt Cecil we wanted to get married. The planning began. We got our marriage license, and we asked the pastor of my home church to marry us after the next Sunday service. I'll never forget how excited I was and how full of hope I was for the future. Despite everything that had already happened, the future looked great. I was marrying the man of my dreams—at least I thought so at the time.

The day of our wedding came. It was a beautiful Sunday morning. David and I came armed with our marriage license, my brother-in-law Andy, and Aunt Cecil. David was dressed in one of the best suits his Aunt Cecil's ever made for him. Yes, Aunt Cecil was a seamstress, as well as our wedding planner, caterer, and bed and breakfast host. I wore a beautiful, baby blue dress Aunt Cecil bought me, and I carried a small blue bouquet. I will never forget that dress. To others, it looked like a nice blue dress, but to me I looked and felt as if I had on a beautiful long wedding gown with a flowing train. A girl can dream, can't she? I don't really remember a word of the sermon Pastor Parks spoke that day. I was so excited and focused on the events coming after service, I could hardly contain myself. Our guest list was small. Pastor Parks told everyone during the announcements that he was marrying a couple after service, and they were all invited. You might say that it was more of a "captured audience" wedding. No bells and whistles, no music or singing, just the music in our heads. After service was over, Pastor Parks called us up to the front of the church. My brother-in-law Andy was the best man and one of the ladies of the church was my maid of honor. Talk about how easy it was not to have to pick and choose who would be my maid of honor. Our wedding was a small, sweet, and simple marriage ceremony. No frills, no bouquet to throw, no reception, and no clue of what was ahead. We were legal and I guess we thought what we didn't know wouldn't hurt us. We were in love and bullet proof.

CHAPTER 2

THE NIGHTMARE YEARS

"Be ye not unequally yoked together
with unbelievers: for what fellowship hath righteousness with unrighteousness? and what communion hath
light with darkness?" — 2 Corinthians
6:14 (NKJV)

ONE OF THE things that many couples say is, "Our
love will keep us together." Well, Tina Turner was
right when she asked the question in her famous song,
"What's Love Got to Do with It?" David and I were
brought together by many sets of circumstances, none
of which were really based on love. The life histories
we brought together were a bunch of events that we
used as just cause for eventually getting married. We
thought we knew love, and that we had experienced
love. We were ready to marry and live happily ever

after. Well, I can say at this point in my life we had no clue what true love was all about. We really didn't know about the right kind of love. The love that God desires us to have, has everything to do with marriage. Unfortunately, couples don't always start out with the right kind of love. The love of God or Agape love, is the only love that can sustain you and not the infatuation or physical attraction kind of love. When infatuation or physical attraction ran out, we were just two people running away from our pasts with the hopes that it would not catch up with us. I am confident that David and I were participating in Eros love. That kind of love was all about passion, and passion was what we had plenty of, most of the time. So yes, Tina, God's divine (Agape) love is what it is all about. Romans 5:8 (NIV) states, "But God demonstrates his own love for us in this: While we were still sinners, Christ died for us." Now, that is true love! The kind of love that is unmerited, unearned, and unconditional. It is the love of God for men that is universal. God's unconditional love transcends and persists regardless of circumstances. Isn't it wonderful to know that God loved us before we were His? It's exciting to know that when we were in our messes, God loved us. Now, that's love, Tina. You see, when we learn that kind of love, then and only then, can we begin to understand God's grace and mercy for us. It is that kind of love we should have for each other as a husband and wife. Our marriages should parallel the relationship we should want and desire to have with God.

The first ten years or so of our marriage would be what we would label as the "Nightmare Years." This time was the period when we started realizing that we were not as compatible as we may have led ourselves to believe. It was the time when little secrets started to creep out. Those secretes became larger than life. David had a problem with drugs, mommy and daddy issues, and the normal dysfunctions that a young man has when there is no man in the home to teach and guide him. I had insecurities, self-esteem issues, and mommy and daddy issues. None of those issues worked well together. David used drugs to make himself feel better about his past. He was the son of a man who couldn't hack life, so, during an argument with his wife, he killed her and then killed himself. On the other hand, I was a young girl of divorced parents who hated each other. They profusely drank alcohol to hide their own pain. David and I were both broken and in pieces and still trying to make something out of nothing at the time. To make matters worse, we threw some kids in with this melting pot of madness, later to find that we had begun to recreate the lives our parents had so graciously left us. We were creating the same dysfunctional family that we both grew up in.

We lived in Atlanta, Georgia, the first years of our marriage. David worked at a company called Siemens

Automation and I worked at the C & S Bank. David started working at a young age, so he really believed in having a job. That was something his Aunt Cecil, who raised him, instilled in him at a young age. Her motto was "If you want to eat, you got to work." She truly meant that in the most literal sense. In fact, I must say that David has worked on a job as far back as I can remember. Although we both worked during our early years of marriage, we did not know how to manage money. You would think that since I worked at a bank, I would have had some knowledge about handling money. Wrong! I did not. In fact, I knew nothing about managing money other than how to spend it. I managed to spend it as I earned it. Wasn't that what money was for? David, on the other hand, had more philanthropic things to spend his money on like marijuana, cocaine, and alcohol. So, between the two of us, we had a lot of good practice with living paycheck to paycheck. As I recall, we lived above and beyond our means, spending money as if it was hot rocks in our hands. It was amazing how we didn't seem to understand or perceive that sooner or later this lifestyle of spending would eventually come to an end. When the children came, we spent more money, and we stop paying our bills. It was almost as if we believed someone was going to "swoop" down and decide to pay them for us. Well, let me tell you right here and now, no one ever comes and pays your bills. In fact, most people who knew about our frivolous lifestyle, sat back, and folded their arms and watched us sink in the world's deepest financial quicksand. Forget what you see in movies about great quicksand rescues. Those type of financial rescues don't happen. The more we squirmed, the deeper we sank. The more money we spent, the deeper we continued to sink.

Our first crisis of money began after we had our first child. Between the three of us, there was no adult in the room. We thought we were living the dream, so we bought our first house. Once again, we failed to understand the importance of budgeting and dealing with those nasty little habits we had. We spent money we didn't have and couldn't understand why the gas, water, and electric companies would not allow us to use their services without paying for them. Even more than this, we still had family issues. If you recall earlier, I referenced David's mother who did not have time for her son. One day, she decided she needed a place to stay along with her other three children. Apparently, no one took the measurements of our house and noted that it was not big enough for a wife, a husband, a child, a mother-in-law, a sister-in-law, and two brothers-in-law. The house was our house, and it was not big enough for all of us. My husband allowed his mother and siblings to move in with us, which probably was the number one cardinal sin of marriage. In-laws and wives do not play nice in one house. The consequence of those choices ended up being the groundwork for the creation of a war zone. There wasn't a demilitarized zone like they had in the Korean War. There was no sacred space, and all weapons were allowed. We did not have physical weapons, but we had an arsenal full of verbal weapons at our disposal. This new world order created the right kind of environment for separation, divorce, and a host of other things. What's more, to make matters worse, David's family did not have any income. No one in the house was paying bills. So, I decided since I could not beat them, I would leave them. That is exactly what I did. Being the independent bruised woman that I was, I took our one child at that time and moved out and left David with his family.

Now, this is probably the place where I tell you that despite all of that, we somehow managed over the years to love each other. We simply did not know how to do this thing called marriage. We didn't have a book to read, a mentor, or anyone who was around to stop us from creating marital suicide. We were lost, and we made emotional decisions based on short-term issues. I guess you might say that absence does make the heart grow fonder. My solo departure was short lived. As it turned out, after a short period of time, David eventually left the family at the house and came and stayed with me. We did not have a plan and neither did David's mother and siblings. The "fam", as I will affectionately call them, did not understand the principle of paying the mortgage if they planned to continue to live in the house. Mortgage companies tend to frown on owners living in homes and not paying. So, our lovely first home was foreclosed on by the mortgage company. After they foreclosed on the home, they wanted everyone to move out. My in-laws had a brief problem with that reality, but the mortgage company seemed to be experts at making people vacate their premises. There was nothing like sitting at the foreclosure table after the bank had taken our home and sold it. They so generously handed us a check for a whopping $48.00, which apparently was an overage on the sale of our home. They handed the check to us like we just won the lottery and looked at us as if we should be grateful for those few dollars we really didn't deserve. We had the joyous pleasure of getting the overage. We didn't know whether to laugh or cry. That was the sum of our accomplishments in our marriage. We had managed to leave the table with $48.00, broke, busted, and disgusted.

Over the next few years or so we continued to pour more salt into the wounds of our marriage. We moved two more times, added another child, and our bills continued to mount. Life is so funny. We were already struggling with one child, but reunions make strange bed fellows and so we had another child. Children are a joy and a rude awakening that you have officially added another person to the group to be miserable. But remember, God has a way of taking care of babies and fools. Despite the additions to our family, and all the bills we had created, we came to that fateful day when we realized if we didn't pay our rent or our utilities, we were going to be homeless. We lived in an apartment complex in Decatur, Georgia, and we found out that most apartment complexes did not have a lot of compassion for you having children when you cannot pay your rent. You know, they agreed that our situation was bad, but they still wanted their money. The utility companies also seemed to have that same mindset. We had two children and we did not want them to be traumatized by our misguided behavior. So, it was about this time that desperation began to set in, and we started devising plans and schemes to outwit the very people who had seen this behavior before in other former tenants. As a special note, you should always remember that someone else had this same plan before you; it didn't work for them, and it probably won't work for you.

One thing is for sure, I found that when you don't know God, desperation can make you come in agreement with the devil when the need arises. He conveniently positions himself to be your best friend. That is not the time you need a friend like Satan. Jesus knew that Satan was not a friend during the time he was tested in the wilderness. In Luke 4:1–13 (KJV), we see where Jesus, full of the Holy Spirit, was led into the wilderness:

> [4] And Jesus answered him, saying, It is written, That man shall not live by bread alone, but by every word of God.

⁵ And the devil, taking him up into an high mountain, shewed unto him all the kingdoms of the world in a moment of time. ⁶ And the devil said unto him, All this power will I give thee, and the glory of them: for that is delivered unto me; and to whomsoever I will I give it. ⁷ If thou therefore wilt worship me, all shall be thine. ⁸ And Jesus answered and said unto him, Get thee behind me, Satan: for it is written, Thou shalt worship the Lord thy God, and him only shalt thou serve. ⁹ And he brought him to Jerusalem, and set him on a pinnacle of the temple, and said unto him, If thou be the Son of God, cast thyself down from hence: ¹⁰ For it is written, He shall give his angels charge over thee, to keep thee: ¹¹ And in their hands they shall bear thee up, lest at any time thou dash thy foot against a stone. ¹² And Jesus answering said unto him, It is said, Thou shalt not tempt the Lord thy God. ¹³ And when the devil had ended all the temptation, he departed from him for a season (Luke 4:1-13).

Jesus took the Word of God as His weapon to fight against the temptations that Satan put before Him. The same power that Jesus used as a Spirit-filled man of God against Satan, was available to us. Fortunately for us, Jesus knew the difference and sent the devil on his way. David and I, on the other hand, didn't quite know the difference between the plans of Satan and the plan of God. When you don't know God, the devil can make you believe that his plan to get you out from under what is happening is a perfect plan. He is always in the details, especially if you don't know God and you are definitely not hearing God's voice. The devil will do everything he can to get you to take him up on his offer to work things out and he will help you with that plan that is designed to sink you deeper into desperation and misery. Keep in mind though, when you are on the path that God knew you would be on, you need to know that God will allow you to run your play all the way out until you run out of room. It is just about the time you get to the end of your rope that our Father so lovingly begins the process of wooing you toward Him. It may not be immediate, but it will happen. You may not feel anything, and you may not see anything at the time, but God is lovingly wooing you. Even though you see bad things happening in your life, those things do not define you and they will not kill you.

Once we came to our ultimate place of desperation, we decided that the best thing for us was to get a U-Haul, pack up our stuff, and steal away in the night—children and all. We headed to the safety of our hometown, Eatonton, Georgia, where David's family lived. No one would know or be able to find us—at least that was what we thought. Did you know that debt will always find you? In fact, I began to believe that debt had its own private investigators who did nothing but look for people just like us who were trying to run away from their pasts, their histories, and their lives. All our creditors found us. Even the ones we least suspected. And of course, the devil was right there sitting happy as he could be, because everything was working out as he planned. Our lives, our marriage, and our family were a mirror image of what we thought we had left behind in our own childhoods. It was like looking in a mirror and seeing your own reflection and not being able to believe that it's you. About this time, I was asking myself, "How did I get to this place?" Why don't I recognize who I am?

Moving back to our hometown was not our best idea. We had to work and that meant we had to drive back and forth to Atlanta to hold onto our jobs. We drove two hundred miles a day. Once again, we didn't have a good plan. When we were stealing away during the night to keep the apartment manager from seeing us, we really didn't have time to lay out a plan. We didn't have time to have contingencies or alternate plans in case the first plan we started on fell apart. Oh, did I mention that we didn't have the best car? Our credit was bad, and we couldn't borrow a dime. The car we had died not too long after we moved back to Eatonton. David's

Aunt Cecil saved the day by cosigning for a new car to handle the drive back-and-forth to Atlanta. It was right about that time we began to convince ourselves, perhaps things were not so bad after all. We had a new car and even though the drive back and forth ate us up in gas money, we were still working things out together. Clearly, we didn't realize we had not gotten out of the quicksand. We had just been holding on to a vine that was about to break and there was no one there to pull us out. We were struggling and struggling in the quicksand until we finally got the revelation that the more, we moved around, the faster we began to sink. I can say that this may have been one of those few times we agreed on something. Our intentions were good, but our ideas were bad. I will say, though, God has a way of stopping the madness in your life when He has a plan for you. He has a way of allowing you to go through chaos and then out of nowhere you see that you are about to have a head on collision with trouble. It is truly like hitting a brick wall—a big brick wall. Sometimes you have minor injuries and other times you have major injuries. Either way, you are going to stop. God now has your undivided attention.

CHAPTER 3

THE DAMASCUS ROAD EXPERIENCE

3 And as he journeyed, he came near Damascus: and suddenly there shined round about him a light from heaven: 4 And he fell to the earth, and heard a voice saying unto him, Saul, Saul, why persecutest thou me? 5 And he said, Who art thou, Lord? And the Lord said, I am Jesus whom thou persecutest: it is hard for thee to kick against the pricks. 6 And he trembling and astonished said, Lord, what wilt thou have me to do? And the Lord said unto him, Arise, and go into the city, and it shall be told thee what thou must do. — Acts 9:3-6

OUR TRAVELS BACK and forth to Atlanta ended abruptly one day with a car accident. Remember that vine in the quicksand I mentioned in the last chapter? Well, it finally broke. Little did we know that our life was about to come to a screeching halt. While driving home one day, we were in a head on collision with not only another automobile, but with life. I woke up a few days later in a hospital with a badly broken leg and a concussion. David appeared to fair well without any major injuries. We had no idea we were on a new trajectory. We were about to go through years of marital transformation. You might say that we were in the midst of our Damascus Road experience. It was almost like the Apostle Paul's experience. One minute, Paul was up terrorizing people and then the next thing he knew he was stunned by a bright light. The book of Acts describes Paul's conversion on the Damascus Road in Acts 9:1–9 (NKJV),

> 9 Then Saul, still breathing threats and murder against the disciples of the Lord, went to the high priest 2 and asked letters from him to the synagogues of Damascus, so that if he found any who were of the Way, whether men or women, he might bring them bound to Jerusalem. 3 As he journeyed he came near Damascus, and suddenly a light shone around him from heaven. 4 Then he fell to the ground, and heard a voice

saying to him, "Saul, Saul, why are you persecuting Me?" [5] And he said, "Who are You, Lord?" Then the Lord said, "I am Jesus, whom you are persecuting. [a] It *is* hard for you to kick against the goads." [6] So he, trembling and astonished, said, "Lord, what do You want me to do?" Then the Lord *said* to him, "Arise and go into the city, and you will be told what you must do." [7] And the men who journeyed with him stood speechless, hearing a voice but seeing no one. [8] Then Saul arose from the ground, and when his eyes were opened he saw no one. But they led him by the hand and brought *him* into Damascus. [9] And he was three days without sight, and neither ate nor drank (Acts 9:1-9).

I want to say hit in the face is how I felt when I woke up in the hospital. Neither David nor I could see that somehow, we had been given another chance. Little did we know, just like the Apostle Paul, we were being set upon another path. This path would be bumpy at first but different from what we had ever experienced.

When you don't know Christ, you don't see a lot of stuff coming. The Apostle Paul didn't see his conversion coming either. He was carrying out business as usual.

He never thought he was going to be seeing light from heaven, let alone hearing voices from heaven. In Acts 9:3-4 (NKJV), it says,

> ³ As he journeyed, he came near Damascus, and suddenly a light shone around him from heaven. ⁴ Then he fell to the ground, and heard a voice saying to him, "Saul, Saul, why are you persecuting Me (Acts 9:3-4)?"

I am not going to say we heard a voice, but I will tell you that the accident changed our lives. Perhaps, there was a light and a voice, and I just don't remember, but whatever it was, it was life changing. Over the next few years, we continued the game of hide and seek with the Lord. God, on the other hand, did what He does best, He set us up for a big play. It was a play where we were at the end of our rope. We were in a place where we did not have any other choice but to follow him. It was the place where we ran out of options, and we had nothing left but to surrender to Him. God always gets His man or woman. He is better than a U.S. Marshal or FBI agent when it comes to getting his man or woman. He has a radar that you can't imagine, and He always starts placing people in your life who you cannot seem to get away from. For David, it was Robbie Sparks. She was a coworker at his job and the President of the local

2131 International Brotherhood of Electrical Workers. She was one of those people who God placed in our lives to drive us nuts. She knew God and she was determined that we would know God. We just could not get away from her and her Jesus. The funny part about it, she and David worked together, and she felt it was her mission to introduce him to Jesus. Imagine an unsaved individual going to work every day and being chased around the plant by their own dedicated evangelist. It drove David nuts. God just knows how to place people in your life to get you to the right place at the right time. Those kinds of people are peskier than mosquitos. They are always buzzing around somewhere, ready to give you a scripture here and there. They are the people we just couldn't seem to get away from.

I would like to tell you though, we only had ten years of turbulence in our marriage, and we lived happily ever after. Unfortunately, the turbulence did not end in ten years. I can remember many days when David would go out into the night, and I had no inkling of when he might return. He was usually fulfilling his insatiable desire to numb the pain of the past and the present with the ultimate weapon of choice, drugs. On the other hand, I began to take on the philosophy of "If you can't beat him, join him." So, I resorted to a more accessible item of choice, alcohol. Since I had come from a family of drinkers, I figured I was already an expert at killing pain. I must say though, I was very fortunate that I didn't end up an alcoholic, but I sure came close to it. Drinking alcohol gave me something to look forward to at the end of each week. That was the way we both tended to fool ourselves into thinking that we didn't have a problem. Since we classified ourselves as weekend users, who could it hurt? We started on Friday and worked our way through Sunday, and we would be all sobered up and ready to go to work on Monday.

Now, you might be asking what happened to the kids? Well, they were fortunate to be surrounded by aunties and cousins who made sure their lives were not destroyed by their parents who had not found themselves. Our children were smart and athletically inclined. With the help of Aunt Cecil and Cousin Emma, they were able to make sure our children were exposed to all the facets of academics and extra-curriculars. They were also very good at keeping our children away from the not so nice street life that many of their friends were experiencing. Although we didn't have a moral compass for our marriage, we did have one for raising our children. If there was any one thing we could agree on, it was raising our children and being there for them even if we could not be there for each other. But God was so amazing. While we were busy destroying ourselves, God was getting ready to throw a wrench in our life, or should I say He was setting up another detour. That detour was going to interrupt our journey and change our direction. I have always been amazed at how fast time can fly by when you are aimlessly going along in life with no real plan or purpose. It is easy to convince yourself that you can make it despite what your life looks like. Remember that the Apostle Paul did not know what hit him until he saw the light and heard the voice of God. God can show up anywhere, anytime, and any place. No matter where you are or what state you are in, when God is ready, or should I say when He has had enough of your foolishness, He shows up. I promise it isn't something you will forget.

I remember how I would leave my children in the bed at night and go venturing out for my beloved husband. This is where you should be asking, "What was I thinking?" I wasn't thinking or at least clearly thinking. I was putting my precious gifts in danger because I always thought I could find their father and fix him. It's funny now when I reflect on all the deals I tried to make with God to fix David. There was never a time that I considered I might need some fixing. Besides, I had put up with a lot over the years, and I thought the least God could do was get David turned around. I needed God to make David do what he was supposed to do as a husband and father and then, our lives would be better. The minor problems that I had did not hold a candle to the myriad of things that God needed to fix in David. Again, it's simply amazing how I thought I was so perfect. I held a mirror up to David and stood behind it so I could not see myself. It was easy to do

31

that, and then I didn't have to look in the mirror and see myself. Then, one night, I sat in my car, in the front yard crying and going on about David and still making deals with the Lord. I begged God to bring David home in one piece all at the same time providing God with a list of additional items I also needed God to fix. I guess I figured that while God was at it, He might as well deal with a total package. I will say though, I didn't see a blinding light, but during the call out of my laundry list, I heard the Lord. His voice was loud and clear. Yes, a clear audible sound deep within my spirit. I heard someone speak to me. I couldn't imagine, amid my long to-do list, God was speaking to me. I once heard my grandmother say God spoke to her, but since I never heard him before, I just assumed that was what grand-mothers say when they are trying to convince you that God is real. So, there I was in my car, in the yard, in the dark, by myself, still looking around to see if there was someone out there in the darkness talking to me. Better yet, I wanted to make sure I wasn't losing it out there in the dark sitting in my car. Well, it was someone talking to me all right. It was my Father in Heaven. It was that same still small voice Elijah heard at Mount Horeb. In 1 Kings 19:11–13 (NKJV) the voice said,

> "Go out, and stand on the mountain before the LORD." And behold, the LORD passed by, and a great and strong

wind tore into the mountains and broke the rocks in pieces before the LORD, but the LORD was not in the wind; and after the wind an earthquake, but the LORD was not in the earthquake; and after the earthquake a fire, but the LORD was not in the fire; and after the fire a still small voice. So, it was, when Elijah heard it, that he wrapped his face in his mantle and went out and stood in the entrance of the cave. Suddenly a voice came to him, and said, "What are you doing here, Elijah (1 Kings 19:11-13)?"

God had taken the liberty to allow me my time of whining, crying, and complaining before He gently let me know that He could fix David and He did not need my help. He didn't need me to provide a laundry list or make recommendations about how to fix him. To my surprise, God was telling me that He needed to fix me. He needed to transform my life in such a way that I would not recognize the old me. He needed me to allow Him into my heart and allow Him to clear away the clutter of my past and become Lord of my life. He already had big plans for David, and I was the final loose end in all of it. God was waiting on me to surrender. I needed to get ready for my new trajectory. God was going to do the one thing I had not asked for and that was to fix me. He was going to repair all the broken places in my life and transform me into a servant for His use. It was the moment when the Potter meets the clay. Jeremiah 18:3–4 (English Standard Version) states, "So I went down to the potter's house, and there he was working at his wheel. And the vessel he was making of clay was spoiled in the potter's hand, and he reworked it into another vessel, as it seemed good to the potter to do." Who would have thought that I would need some fixing? Well, you can best believe God thought about it and He wasn't taking "no" for an answer.

Chapter 4

Metamorphosis

17 Therefore if any man be in Christ, he
is a new creature: old things are passed
away; behold, all things are become
new.— 2 Corinthians 5:17 (KJV)

THE MERRIAM-WEBSTER ONLINE dictionary
defines the word "transformation" as a "major change
in the appearance or character of someone or something." When we accept Jesus Christ as Lord and Savior
of our lives, we begin the process of transforming. We
become a new creation and all the old things in our lives
go away. A brand-new life emerges. This fact means
that with Christ, we get a choice to run toward sin or
run away from sin. With Christ, we become perfect,
like Him, so we may enter Heaven. The funny thing is,
transformation is truly a process. We start out one way,

but then over time we become something else. If we take the path of Christ, we become a new creation, and all things become new.

Our transformation is like the butterfly. It begins its life as a caterpillar. It has one job in life and that is to eat. Caterpillars face tremendous challenges as they grow. The first thing is a caterpillar's skin cannot grow with it. So, for a caterpillar to grow larger than the skin it has, it must make a new, larger skin. The caterpillar, also called a larva, is a long creature that looks like a worm. Once hatched, the caterpillar immediately starts to eat the leaf it was born on, and the flowers around it. This process is called the eating and growing stage. Although a caterpillar is small when it is born, it starts to grow relatively fast because it eats all the time. Its accelerated growth causes the caterpillar to become too big for its skin, which causes it to have to shed its old skin. It then gets a new skin, and this process continues at least four or more times while it is in the growing stage. In the third stage, or chrysalis, all growth stops. The caterpillar is in a resting and changing stage. The caterpillar starts to look different, and its shape starts to quickly change. This stage creates a butterfly. In the last and final stage, the chrysalis opens, and the butterfly makes its grand appearance. Although the butterfly cannot fly well at first, it doesn't take long before it learns and then it flies free.

So, our lives are just like the caterpillar. We have a sin nature or a spiritually unregenerated heart when we are born. The sin nature is the aspect that makes a man rebel against God. So, when we speak of sin nature, we refer to the fact that we have a natural inclination to sin. If we are given the choice to do God's will or to follow our own desires, we will naturally choose to do our own thing. It's that sin nature that will lead us to hell if we don't accept Jesus Christ as Lord and Savior of our lives. It's this transformation that allows us to exchange that spiritually unregenerated heart for a new heart to become a new creature in Christ Jesus. What a wonderful exchange, to be better than you were and to have an expectation of a glorious and abundant life. That's the joy in Jesus!

I believe we began to witness transformation after David attended a T.D. Jakes men's conference. I can't say why this moment or why this time. God has such a sense of humor when He goes about weaving in between the lines to change the trajectory of your life. David was invited to attend a T.D. Jakes' conference. I was not as excited about the concept of him attending the conference because his past practice had shown me that he couldn't always be trusted. Perhaps, it was more about the fact that I didn't want to have one more disappointment added to my plate of disappointments. I didn't want to have a hope and desire that this time would be different. I didn't even really care about who he was going with. I just didn't want to get my hopes up and be disappointed one more time. In the book of Hebrews 11:1 (NKJV), the Word of God says, "Now faith is the substance of things hope for and the evidence of things not seen." The idea is that we believe God without evidence. My transformation needed to include trusting God and leaning not to my own understanding. I needed to learn to trust God for my man. I needed to learn, that because I didn't see it, didn't mean that God wasn't on duty working behind the scenes. He was transforming David and He was transforming me. God was teaching me to focus on Him and He would take care of the rest. When David told me he was going to that conference, my fears and anxiety began to react instead of my faith. I didn't trust and I didn't believe. Sometimes, God must blow your mind to change your mind. Against my better judgement, David went to that T.D. Jakes' conference and the metamorphosis began. When he returned home that night, he informed me that Jesus had pleaded his case and found him not guilty. I accepted his statement with my usual consternation, but what I didn't know was that God was now in the driver's seat and the change had begun. The caterpillar began to shed its old skin.

I won't tell you that things in my marriage and my home changed overnight, but I will tell you that the thing I had cried, begged, and pleaded for was happening. It wasn't just happening to David; it was happening to me, too. I was shedding my old skin and experiencing my metamorphosis. I was being changed from within. God had been there all the time prepping me for my new change. He was wearing me down to a point of surrender. I finally yielded enough for the Master to work. My prayers for God to change David morphed into asking God to change me and make me what He created me to be. I was the clay on the potter's wheel being molded and shaped for His use. For the first time, I saw God for myself. It wasn't about David any longer, it was about me, and the transformation that I needed.

As the years passed, we began to go to a church nearby, and it fed a hunger and thirst as never before. God's Word came alive in our hearts and minds, and we began to see ourselves, and each other, as vessels of God for His use. I became a member of the choir and David eventually became a Junior Deacon on the Deacon Board. Of all things, who would have thought! When God puts His mighty hand on you, nothing is impossible. I could never have imagined myself singing in a choir, let alone directing one. David on the Deacon Board was a miracle all by itself. I never imagined that the guy who was a drug user could become a Junior Deacon. Who would have thought it was possible? Who would have thought we could be in a church? it was just the beginning. God had just warmed up. He set the stage for His next move. We were a family going to church and living a life that was worthy of the gracious and merciful God whom we served. God set us up for the next phase of our metamorphosis—another layer of skin was about to shed.

After attending a nearby church for a few years, David got his call from God to the ministry. David never imagined that God would choose him of all people. I never thought it either. In fact, I did ask God a few times if He really knew what He was doing. I mean, being called into the ministry was a leap from Junior Deacon. That's where we got it wrong. 1 Corinthians 1:27, (NKJV) states, "But God has chosen the foolish things of the world to put to shame the wise, and God has chosen the weak things of the world to put to shame the things which are mighty." What seemed foolish to us or didn't make sense to us, made perfect sense to God. God chooses people who don't socially qualify but spiritually qualify. He chooses people who are counted out by men. He chooses people like Abraham. You know, the man who was later known as the Father of Many Nations? Although he was included in the hall of fame of faith, he was far from being a man who kept the faith. God promised to give Abraham a child. Unfortunately, Abraham and Sarah decided to take matters into their own hands and work the promise of God out through their servant Hagar. Regardless, God stayed faithful and gave Abraham the promise. Then, there was Samson who was not the most reliable or obedient guy.

Regardless of his hard headedness and arrogance, God gave him supernatural strength through the power of the Holy Spirit. Even after he fell because of his sinfulness and lust toward Delilah, God brought His purpose to pass through Samson. Then, we have Moses. He was considered a coward and a murderer but eventually the man that God chose to lead His people out of the land of Egypt to the Promise Land. This person is the guy who claimed he couldn't speak very well, and God took away his excuses. Man would have crossed him off the list, but God used him anyhow. Finally, we have Peter, one of Jesus' disciples. Peter was an impulsive kind of guy who lacked courage. He talked too much and spoke too fast, but he was restored by Jesus and filled with the Holy Spirit. How many people do you know like Peter? Personally, I kind of felt I acted like that. You know, quick at the mouth and not big enough to back it up. I always wondered why the smallest people always have the most mouth. Nevertheless, Peter was considered one of the greatest apostles of all time because he had a powerful public ministry. So, you see, God doesn't pick the people we think have it all together. He picks the people who have messed up in life and who can tell us about getting a second chance. You know, someone who has walked a mile in our shoes. Who better to have a great testimony about transformation and the goodness of God? It's the foolish things that confound the wise.

CHAPTER FIVE

MONEY AND SEX MATTERS

"No man can serve two masters: for either he will hate the one, and love the other; or else he will hold to the one, and despise the other. Ye cannot serve God and mammon."—Matthew 6:24 (KJV)

MANAGING YOUR FINANCES is a job all by itself. Many couples tend to come into their marriages with a yours and mine attitude when it comes down to the financial resources they will have in the marriage. Fighting over money, and the lack thereof, can take even the strongest couple down the road to divorce. Couples get married and continue to live the life of a single without any idea about how much money and debt they have. They are in a financial downfall before they realize what has happened. Once spouses realize they are in a no-win financial situation, they take on part-time jobs or seek out other means of making more money to try to get out of debt. Conversations between couples take on the form of blaming each other for the financial problems or discovering debt that was never discussed at the beginning of the marriage.

According to Dave Ramsey, in Ramsey Solutions Study, "Nearly two-thirds of all marriages start off in debt. Forty-three percent of couples married more than 25 years started off in debt, while 86 percent of couples married five years or less started off in the red—twice the number of their older counterparts. One-third of people who say they argued with their spouse about money say they hid a purchase from their spouse because they knew their partner would not approve (Dave Ramsey, 2018)."

We didn't have any money management or financial stewardship conversations at the beginning of our marriage. Although we married with no debt, I did not have a job. David's income was the only income in our household. We had not given any thought to how we would pay for rent, groceries, or anything else. We were infatuated with each other and the conversations about money didn't tend to come up at first. In fact, the attitude in most cases was "us against the world." Little did we know that there were many things we would need to pay for in this world and our love was not going to be enough. Once again, as I said earlier, when we reflect on what Tina Turner said in her hit song "What's Love Got to Do with It," I can answer that question now with certainty as it relates to money, "not a thing Tina." Love will not and does not pay the bills. In fact, if anything, many couples will say they loved each other very much but they just couldn't handle always being without money, debtors calling, arguments, and a total loss of control of their finances. Eventually, they abandoned ship, went their separate ways, and put their stakes down somewhere else.

David and I got the rude awakening that we were going to need more than just our love. After a few months of fairytale living, we had no choice. I had to start looking for a job. Now keep in mind, the world was still rotating on its axis. Many jobs were requiring that we had at least a college degree if we wanted to make the kind of money that we believed we needed to make. So, simply being a high school graduate meant that we would pretty much be working on the bottom rung of the workforce. We knew working an entry level job would mean making just the minimum wage. David worked for an electrical apparatus company, and I started working at a bank. I had no concept of how much things cost and neither did David. Most of David's childhood experiences as it relates to money came from his Aunt Cecil. Aunt Cecil knew that a person who did not work did not eat. I got my education regarding money from my grandparents. My grandfather had his own business, and my grandmother was a retired teacher. My world, at that time, consisted of my grandfather being the breadwinner and my grandmother just living at home fat and happy. Now, we are talking about the early 70s when that kind of life was possible. Unfortunately, for David, everyone in his family worked and there were no fat and happy people at home. I really didn't understand the difference between my grandparent's life in the early 60s and 70s and our life in the 80s and 90s. The dream world I lived in basically said anything I wanted I could have. Boy was I wrong. Although I had worked a few years, I knew nothing about budgets or stewardship. What I knew about budgeting and finance would not feed me or my family.

I must say, David's home life was much different from my home life. His aunt was single. She worked in manufacturing, and she worked very hard to raise a young man in the early 70s. David worked at an early age because in his aunt's house there were no free rides. Although David was raised to have a strong work ethic, there was not a lot of focus on how to budget and save. The pattern he saw in his home was get all you can and work several jobs to pay for it if you really wanted it bad enough. That sounds fine when you do not want much, but when you begin to see what others have, you want everything. Of course, wanting everything is fine until you can't pay for it. Children and cars are very expensive. You just decide one day that it would be nice to have one until those wonderful jewels get here and then the question of the day is, "How will we pay for them?" Now, I know there has always been the saying "the Lord will provide," but first we needed to know the Lord and then we could have the faith He would provide. We were going through the financial jungle without a map or guide. It was not long before we realized we had a mess, and we were moving in the middle of the night as I mentioned earlier. We were trying to get ahead of the debt police that was on our trail because we just didn't have the financial resources to save ourselves.

In the book of Ecclesiastes 4:9–10a (NIV) the scripture, states, "Two are better than one, because they have a good return for their labor: If either of them falls down, one can help the other up." If we apply this scripture to marriage, we can begin to understand that the Word of God shows us that when a husband and wife come together and put their resources together, they can get a great return for their labor. When we sit down and lay all our cards on the table and work to create a budget, we can begin to see how we can make our money work for us and not against us. Often in marital relationships financial failure is due, in part, to poor stewardship and failure to work together. We must learn how to be good stewards over that which God has given us stewardship. Biblical principles about debt are no good to us if we don't know them and we aren't able to apply them. It is important to know the actual income that each one in the marriage makes. Couples need to know how much outstanding debt they have, if they have insurance, if they have any assets, and if they are co-signers on any loans. What's more, they need to know if they have large amounts of student loan debt. All things financial should be discussed.

Living within our means is an essential component as it relates to unity in our finances. It is important to ensure that what we spend each month is less than or equal to the amount of money we bring into our household each month. Knowing the difference between our wants, our needs, and our desires is vitally important. Our needs are the purchases that are necessary to provide our basic requirements, such as food, clothing, home, medical coverage, and other things such as transportation, communication devices and computers. We must be careful that we do not mistakenly categorize certain items as needs which are wants. Sometimes, our wants are so powerful, we cannot imagine living without them. The needs that are wants can present themselves as things that help you live more comfortably, but they are not necessarily essential for you to live.

Our wants involve the choices we make about the quality of goods we desire. A want is something that you don't really need, but it will make your life a little better. Some examples of wants versus needs would be dress clothes versus work clothes, steak versus hamburger or a new car versus a used car. All these things fall into the category of the things we want, but do not necessarily have to have. It is vital that we resist the pressure to have the same things as the people around us may have. In 1 Peter 3:3–4 (NKJV) it states, "Do not let your adornment be merely outward—arranging the hair, wearing gold, or putting on fine apparel—rather let it be the hidden person of the heart, with the incorruptible beauty of a gentle and quiet spirit, which is very precious in the sight of God." Peter reminded us here in this passage of scripture that it is important we understand, our beauty comes from within. God doesn't look for how we dress or keep up with the Joneses; He looks for what is inside our hearts. 1 Peter 3:4 (NKJV) says, "'rather let it be the hidden person of the heart, with the incorruptible beauty of a gentle and quiet spirit, which is very precious in the sight of God." So, it doesn't mean that we can't have our wants, but it does mean that keeping up with the latest trends or what other people are doing should not be our number one priority.

Finally, our desires are the choices according to God's plan that we can make only out of the surplus funds after all other necessary obligations have been met. In 1 John 2:15–16 (NKJV) it says, "Do not love the world or the things in the world. If anyone loves the world, the love of the Father is not in him. For all that is in the world—the lust of the flesh, the lust of the eyes, and the pride of life—is not of the Father but is of the world." John instructed us that we should not be overly attached to worldly (non-spiritual) things. We are to love God and one another and not the possessions of the world. The idea here is that if we love things then we cannot love God. We often hear people misuse the Bible scripture in 1 Timothy 6:10 (KJV), which states, "For the love of money is the root of all evil.". Most people drop off the first few words of that scripture and go right to the "money is the root of all evil" part. I ask you to think back to how many times you have heard this verse misquoted. It is the love of money that gets us in trouble. Our attitude toward money is the problem, not the money itself. As I mentioned earlier, we didn't have any sense of stewardship, so it is no wonder that along with our other issues, we began the steep decline toward debt, bad credit, foreclosure, and bankruptcy.

The world is filled with a wealth of obstacles to good planning or money management. Our desire to fulfill our social pleasures quickly led us to become financially overextended. The idea that more was better, regardless of how much it cost, was a crazy notion. When we used credit to delay vital decisions with no additional savings available to cope with rising prices and unexpected expenses, we were setting ourselves up for financial failure. Many times, we tended to offset increases in our income by increasing the level of spending. Unfortunately, if you have poor stewardship, your outcome will be the same.

In the early years of our marriage, we threw money out the window, like you pour water out of a pail. We were very good at spending money with no reality of what it meant. After years of very poor stewardship and our midnight run to Eatonton Georgia, it all came crashing down. We were finally forced to file chapter thirteen bankruptcy. During that time, bankruptcy was the "go to" when you wanted to get out from under an enormous cloud of debt. Unfortunately, when we filed for bankruptcy, we didn't hear the part about the seven years or more we couldn't finance a candy bar. We had no way to get anything other than going to the "we finance" companies for cars, furniture, and anything else we needed. Those companies were ready, willing, and able to meet our needs for an outrageous interest rate or finance charge. Remember I mentioned how desperation can make you do some crazy things? Well, we started going to those finance companies with a willingness to pay whatever they wanted for the rest of our lives. I remember buying a Curtis Mathis television that was probably worth about three hundred dollars. I would bet we paid thirteen hundred dollars for the television during the time we had it. Fortunately, a lightning storm put us out of our misery and struck our house and the television. The insurance on the house paid the last few dollars we owed on the television. I know we bought the television three or four times over. In fact, the television had depreciated, and it was worth about fifty dollars when it did die. Back in the day, many of those companies preyed on people who had bad credit and no money. The mark up on the merchandise was ridiculous, but they knew we were desperate to have whatever it was, and we had no other way of getting it.

David and I spent about thirteen years under the cloud of bankruptcy. We couldn't buy anything in our name because of our bad debt. David's Aunt Cecil had to help us get a mobile home to live in after living with her for some time. When God begins the process of transformation, nothing stays the same. Although it took several years, just as the caterpillar's old skin began to shed, we began to shed the enormous amount of debt we had accumulated. God introduced us to financial planning and stewardship. He showed us in Psalm 24:1 (KJV), "The earth is the LORD's, and the fulness thereof; the world, and they that dwell therein." The reality was, we didn't own anything. Everything in the earth belonged to God and he showed us we were just stewards on this earth and our job was to do what Genesis 1:26 (KJV) states, "And God said, Let us make man in our image, after our likeness: and let them have dominion over the fish of the sea, and over the fowl of the air, and over the cattle, and over all the earth, and over every creeping thing that creepeth upon the earth." God was teaching us what he taught Adam. He was teaching us to have dominion over the earth.

Now, remember that two of the biggest things that couples fight about are money and sex. Surprisingly, you would wonder why in the world would couples argue about sex. It's one of the finer pleasures of married life. Well, unfortunately, sex can be a benefit of being married or it can be weaponized to destroy a marriage. Let me start by saying, how we view sex is based on our exposure and understanding. If growing up, sex was considered a taboo, nasty, or a great secret, our view of the act alone in marital relationships could be perceived in the same manner. As a child, I remember that even mentioning the word sex would get me a knock in the mouth. I lived with my grandparents, and I can tell you that sex was never mentioned or heard of in our house as far as they were concerned. If my grandmother and grandfather had sex, I never knew it. My grandparents were in their early 70s and during the late 60s and early 70s, the word "sex" was taboo. Young girls during that time, who were supposedly out having sex outside of marriage, would have been tagged with some not so nice names. Besides, when you think about it, I believed I would have been grossed out to think that my grand momma and granddaddy were having sex in the next room. Now, of course, while hanging out with my friends we all had our own ideas about sex—what it was, and what it looked like. My recollection of a sex conversation was the one I had with my father. It was short and sweet and to the point. His words to me were very simple, "Don't do it"! I will say, it took me a few years and some experimentation to figure out what I was not supposed to do. I can remember when I was a teenager that we had a storage house in the backyard. I remember seeing my father one night taking a female he was dating into that storage house. Well, it didn't take a rocket scientist to figure out whatever was happening in that house was always done covertly and under the cover of darkness. Being an inquisitive teenager, I managed one day to find my way outside and inside this covert hideaway to find a bed. What a shock! I later found out that it was not good for me to ask my father why the bed was in the storage house. It was off limits to everyone, especially me. Asking about the bed was dead giveaway, I had broken the rule. Later, I shared my discovery with my friends. We determine that sex was covert. It was a secret, it was nasty, and you didn't have to do it with your husband or wife. Clearly, we determined the act itself was not sacred to marriage. It was a feel-good experience that held no other value than the physical experience itself. It is experiences like those, we take with us as we grow into maturity.

Our past sexual experiences or encounters shape what we know and understand about sex. Unfortunately, based on our past experiences we may not have the right knowledge of what purpose sex holds in the marriage. Since it was a secret during my life growing up, you can imagine that trial and error were my teaching tools. I didn't have a parent who took the time to talk to me about this act or expression of intimacy that God gave to married couples. So, as an adult, I didn't have a real understanding about sex other than it felt good, and let's face it, it was a repeatable activity especially when you got married. I can tell you I found out very early how sex can be weaponized by women when they want their way. It can be a great motivator for the wrong reasons. This thinking was not exactly what God intended sex to be. This idea goes back to my point of how we fail to have the right knowledge about sex and its purpose. You can best believe, once I found out how much David wanted sex and that he would just about do anything to get it, I weaponized it. Now, yes, I knew that sex was also for the purposes of procreation, but I knew how to wield my power of holding out. I knew that I wasn't going to get whatever it was I wanted if I didn't hold out. Once again, it was my limited knowledge that made me act that way.

In Genesis 1:28 (NIV), the word of God states, "God blessed them and said to them, 'Be fruitful and increase in number; fill the earth.'" We can see that at the beginning of the creation of men, God's purpose for sex in marriage was to reproduce the human species. Mankind was given a desire for sex, which would make populating the earth probable. Man's job was to exercise his dominion over the earth and populate the earth for the plan of God to be fulfilled. Man was to bond together in a one-flesh relationship. Additionally, God developed sexual expression to help couples develop intimacy. It was created to meet physical and emotional needs. In 1 Corinthians 7:3–5 (NIV), the Apostle Paul spoke to this point when he said:

> The husband should fulfill his marital duty to his wife, and likewise the wife to her husband. The wife's body does not belong to her alone, but also to her husband. In the same way, the husband's body does not belong to him alone but also to his wife. Do not deprive each other except by mutual consent and for a time, so that you may devote yourselves to prayer. Then come together again so that Satan will not tempt you because of your lack of self-control (1 Corinthians 7:3-5).

This is probably where I went wrong. First, I didn't know about this passage and second, I didn't realize that while I weaponized sex, I gave place to the enemy. Satan was probably delighted that I took that position. It would not be too hard for him to set the stage for adultery or anything else he could conjure up. You see, our ignorance of the Word of God can cause us some serious pitfalls. We do things that sabotage our relationships and then try to blame the other spouse. Little did I know that I provided ammunition for extramarital behavior. I'm sure, I would have blamed David for falling prey to his lustful desires, but the realty was I would have been the culprit in that situation. Listen, the scriptures tell us flat out that it is wrong to withhold from each other. By our own behavior, we set the stage for sexual immorality. Hebrews 13:4 (NIV) states, "Marriage should be honored by all, and the marriage bed kept pure, for God will judge the adulterer and all the sexually immoral." Once again, another passage of scripture showing where the Bible celebrates sex as an expression of married love, but as a relationship between husband and wife, which should be pure, holy, and good before God. The enemy of this world works diligently to encourage sex outside of the marriage bed and discourage sex inside the marriage bed. The Apostle Paul reminds us in 1 Corinthians 6:18–20 (NIV) to,

> "Flee from sexual immorality. All other sins a person commits are outside the body, but whoever sins sexually, sins against their own body. Do you not know that your bodies are temples of the Holy Spirit, who is in you, whom you have received from God? You are not your own; you were bought at a price.

> Therefore, honor God with your bodies
> (1 Corinthians 6:18-20)."

Paul told us to flee from sexual immorality. Get away from it! Don't set yourself up for the fall. We must remember that as Christians we are the temple of the Holy Spirit. God Himself lives in us. That means we have the power and the strength over our flesh living right inside of us. Who better to help us fight against this lustful flesh? When we deny physical affection and sexual intimacy to our spouse, we cheat them out of what is due to them. Depriving our spouses in either sense promotes the idea for the deprived to look elsewhere for fulfillment, which leads to the destruction of the marriage. Keep in mind that marriages end for other reasons, but sex happens to be one of the biggest reasons for infidelity or divorce. Spouses turn to infidelity to fill a physical or emotional void left unfilled by their spouse.

Not to give you all the details, but our sex life was pretty good. So, holding out was punishment for myself. Keep in mind that when you deprive your spouse, you are also depriving yourself. It's not just your spouse that can be tempted by Satan, you can too! So, it is vital that we learn to keep all things in perspective. God never intended for us to go outside of the marriage bed and become loose and wild with others. He intended for our marital relationship to mirror our relationship with him. He gave us intimacy to fulfill his ultimate plan. I learned later in life from some very wise older women that I was just setting myself up for failure. Remember, we should give no place to the enemy, and we should do as 1 Thessalonians 5:22 (KJV) says, "abstain from all appearance of evil." Satan uses our desire for pleasure and perverts it for our destruction. I found out that I could ask God to help me approach situations and circumstances in my marriage without everything being a negotiation. God desired for sexual relationship with my husband to be pure, holy, and special. He did not desire for sex to be treated like a reward for good behavior. Sex is an intimate and beautiful aspect of marriage, created by God for husbands and wives to enjoy.

CHAPTER SIX

SUBMISSION IS ALL ABOUT YOUR ATTITUDE

> ²¹ Submitting yourselves one to another in the fear of God. ²² Wives, submit yourselves unto your own husbands, as unto the Lord. ²³ For the husband is the head of the wife, even as Christ is the head of the church: and he is the saviour of the body. ²⁴ Therefore as the church is subject unto Christ, so let the wives be to their own husbands in everything. — Ephesians 5:21–24 (KJV)

IN EPHESIANS 5:22-33 (KJV), the Word of God gives us instructions for the Christian household. It says:

> ²² Wives, submit yourselves unto your own husbands, as unto the Lord. ²³ For

the husband is the head of the wife, even as Christ is the head of the church: and he is the saviour of the body [24] Therefore as the church is subject unto Christ, so let the wives be to their own husbands in everything. [25] Husbands, love your wives, even as Christ also loved the church, and gave himself for it; [26] That he might sanctify and cleanse it with the washing of water by the word, [27] That he might present it to himself a glorious church, not having spot, or wrinkle, or any such thing; but that it should be holy and without blemish. [28] So ought men to love their wives as their own bodies. He that loveth his wife loveth himself. [29] For no man ever yet hated his own flesh; but nourisheth and cherisheth it, even as the Lord the church: [30] For we are members of his body, of his flesh, and of his bones. [31] For this cause shall a man leave his father and mother, and shall be joined unto his wife, and they two shall be one flesh. [32] This is a great mystery: but I speak concerning Christ and the church. [33] Nevertheless let every one of you in particular so love his wife even as

himself; and the wife see that she rever-
ence her husband (Ephesians 5:22-33).

These are probably ten or more disputed or challenging verses of scripture in the Bible for many women.
In fact, I must say in the beginning of my marriage
the word "submission" was not a consideration. I can
remember thinking that David needed to be glad that
I was married to him—let alone submitting to him. At
that time, I was not in any mood to submit to a guy
who did not appear to be able to find his way out of
a lighted room. Unfortunately, I did not realize that
these scriptures were not something written in passing
by some man who knew nothing about women. They
were instructions for what my role was as a wife. You see,
these scriptures were God's command to wives on how
we must submit to our husbands as the church submits
to Christ. The problem is the average woman does not
quite get the understanding that submission is all about
our attitude. According to the Strong's Concordance,
the Greek word for submission is Hypotassō, which is
a Greek military term meaning "to arrange [troop divi-
sions] in a military fashion under the command of a
leader." In non-military use, it was "a voluntary attitude
of giving in, cooperating, assuming responsibility, and
carrying a burden (Strong's Concordance-Blue Letter
Bible, 2022)" The idea here is that we put ourselves
under another person, or we make ourselves subject

to another, or we submit ourselves to the control of another. Of course, in my oh so fleshly mind, I did not understand what it meant to submit to someone, not to mention how to submit to one another. As a woman, I could see myself draw back from the idea of submission, fearing that it would lead to unhealthy control or even violence in our relationship. Submission does not mean that one is weaker, or one should be mistreated because of submitting to the other. Submission means having an attitude and lifestyle of serving one another. One who is submissive does not have to concern themselves with fighting for their equal rights or demanding equal treatment. God, in His infinite wisdom, has ordained the order in the home to parallel that of the church. As male and female, we are to reflect the image of God. It is in that image that we can see how Jesus voluntarily submitted to the Father. John 5:30 (KJV) states, "I can of mine own self do nothing: as I hear, I judge: and my judgment is just; because I seek not mine own will, but the will of the Father which hath sent me." So, just as Jesus submitted to hanging on the cross, the Father wills that we should submit one to another. Our act of submission in the home to our husbands pleases God. We are not only pleasing God, but we are also obeying God's command to submit to our husbands as we submit unto Him. God has made our husbands the head of the household as Christ is the head of the church. So, our attitude should always be to please God.

What I didn't know at the time, was when I failed to submit as God has commanded, I was fulfilling the plan of Satan to walk in disobedience. There can be no success in our relationship unless we follow the established divine arrangement God has set up for us. We should desire to have a life that can be rich and fulfilling that honors God with our submissive obedience.

Now, by no means are men left out of this perfect plan that God has laid out for us. Ephesians 5:21 states that we should "Submit to one another as we submit to Christ." Not only do husbands have a role in this divine arrangement, but they are held accountable by God in Ephesians 5:23, which states, "For the husband is the head of the wife as Christ is the head of the church, his body, of which he is the Savior." Husbands are accountable and responsible for what we do. Once I got the submission thing down, I really liked the idea that David was the one who was responsible for what took place in our home. Now, that didn't mean I could act any kind of way, but it took the pressure off trying to be the head honcho in our relationship by calling the shots. I finally got the revelation that God's perfect plan could work to my benefit if I allowed it. If I took the time to humble myself before the Lord, His unmerited favor would lift me up. You see, what we as women tend to do is take matters into our own hands when we do not think our husbands are working fast enough. Once we get ahead of our husbands, submission goes out the window. I can remember being so disrespectful to my husband during the early years of our marriage. I thought it was my duty and responsibility to keep the ship up right and ensure we did not sink because of all his misdeeds and failures. I saw nothing I did wrong and prided myself at making sure things in the home stayed afloat. I failed to realize that taking the lead in the household did not help matters but made them worse. It was easy to see other people's problems while I ignored my own problems. Jesus said it best in Matthew 7:3 (NIV), "Why do you look at the speck of sawdust in your brother's eye and pay no attention to the plank in your own eye?" Yes, I was very good at not seeing the issues I had when it came to looking at the problems in our marriage. As I look back at things now, it is no wonder things constantly went wrong. In fact, our ship sank regardless of my actions because I was in the wrong position as a wife.

Submission really goes to the core of a woman's behavior in a marital relationship. If we see ourselves as a servant and not as a "helpmate" then our behavior sets the stage for a lot of conflict. I never realized how disrespectful I had become in our marriage. I totally missed God's true intentions for submission. My attitude and understanding of submission were faulty, which was evident in my behavior. Oftentimes, the problem for many couples is there are no role models in their families. I didn't have the type of role model in my family to teach me and show me how I should operate in marriage. What I had was the "if you want something done right, do it yourself" program running in my household. By the time I started living with my grandmother and grandfather, disobedience, and rebellion were well indoctrinated in me. After seeing my parents fight like wrestlers in a cage match, I was determined not to allow that to happen to me. Unfortunately, I set myself on the path of a self-fulfilling prophecy of rebellion and disobedience. There were times where I didn't like something David did, or the way things were going, and I spared no words in telling him. Oh, and I did this generally with an audience. I guess I thought he would not cross me again if I did that. The problem with that behavior was I was making David hate being with me and he was becoming bitter and resentful of the way I handled things. Proverbs 21:9, (NIV) states, "Better to live on a corner of the roof than share a house with a quarrelsome wife." It never dawned on me at the time that I was that quarrelsome wife. There was never anything right in the house and, I certainly did not think I was the reason.

When we usurp our authority in the home, we are in direct rebellion of the plan of God. David could never be the man God wanted him to be if I was in the way issuing demands. Little did I know that I was killing my own destiny as well. One thing about the wonderful Father that we have is that He will not allow us to derail His plan. Sooner or later, He begins to start moving and shifting things into the right place. If you recall, during my Damascus Road experience, God finally gave me that heart to heart I needed regarding my behavior. Just as a loving Father does, He put me in a place where I had to listen. He put me in a place where my options ran out. He put me in a place where I was finally sick and tired of what was happening to my family. The one thing I feared the most became a reality. I turned my own home into the same battle ground that I declared I would never have. God so mercifully turned the mirror on me so I could see what I had become. He also showed me what I could become. I could be a Proverbs 31:10 woman, "a wife of noble character worth far more than rubies." He showed me that He never intended for me to carry my marriage, but I had to allow Him to put the pieces back together and show David and I a better way. I had to allow my heavenly Father to be God in my life. I had to allow Him to make the crooked things in my life straight and the rough places smooth. I had to allow Him to do the molding and shaping of our characters. All I had to do was surrender all to Him and allow Him to direct my path. You see, I had come to a place of brokenness, and I needed God to step in and I needed Him to do it soon so that we would not make our children replicas of what we hated so much in each other.

I remember asking God where He was all that time? He quietly spoke to me and said He had always been there. I was simply so busy running things, and handling things, and getting folks straighten out that I did not notice the times that He carried me when I could not carry myself. I didn't see God in the situations of my life that should have taken me out. Yes, He was there all along waiting on me to be open to receive Him. He reminded me of that while I was out in the streets looking for David, He took care of my children and didn't allow them to perish because of my reckless and careless behavior. He waited on me to say I had enough, and I needed His help.

I can say now what a weight it all was and how good it felt to just let go and let God. Instead of walking around with a dark cloud over my head, I could see sunshine peering into my life. I could see the love that God had for me. I could understand how He loved me so much that He sent His son to die for me, so I would not suffer. God gave me the love I needed as a child, and still needed as an adult and as a parent. I could accept Him unconditionally because that is the way He accepted me. In Hosea 10:12 (NLT) it says, "Plant the good seeds of righteousness, and you will harvest a crop of love. Plow up the hard ground of your hearts, for now is the time to seek the LORD, that he may come and shower righteousness upon you." God could plow up my heart and begin substituting the dark and dirty things of life with His overwhelming love. God taught me how to submit to Him and it is through those lessons (His Word) that I learned to submit to David.

I can tell you this, once you embrace the idea that submission is all about your attitude, you begin to see what you have been missing. You start to see how much stress you put on yourself because you operated outside of your role. I learned how to pray for my husband, rather than dishing out orders and being critical of his every action. I learned how God did not need my help to mold and shape David. He just needed me to be obedient and faithful. He needed me to close my mouth. Women have far more words in their vocabulary than men, so I needed to practice the art of being quiet and allow God to do His thing. As I became more focused on myself and allowed the Word of God to permeate every part of me, I saw the man that God wanted me to have. I saw God downloading His love and care, remodeling David into the man I always desired. I saw God downloading His wisdom in him and smoothing out the rough edges. I saw how my husband needed my help and not my condemnation. Romans 8:1 (KJV) states, "There is therefore now no condemnation to them which are in Christ Jesus, who walk not after the flesh, but after the Spirit." When you walk after the Spirit, you will not get hung up on fleshly things of the world. God let us know through the Apostle Paul that all of God's condemning wrath and his unlimited power against us in our sin were replaced by His mercy and his unlimited powerful assistance. So how in the world could I condemn David if Jesus did not condemn us for our many failures as husband and wife? In fact, it was a good feeling when things were not going particularly right. I could warmly ask David, "So what are you and God going to do about that?" Although it was funny, it was refreshing. Somebody else could figure things out instead of me. What a break. Finally, I yielded my unrelenting place of power and manipulation over my husband. David took his proper position as the man of his home. Now, let me just say, we had plenty of trials and errors, and yes, I had to daily ask the Holy Spirit to guard my tongue. But it was a wonderful thing to see God work in our lives. Just as the potter gently molds and shapes the clay on the wheel, God molded and shaped us. He got us ready for the assignment ahead. It would be an assignment we never imagined God would give to us.

Chapter Seven

Yes, God's Got Jokes

"For many are called, but few are
chosen." — Matthew 22:14 (NKJV)

THERE ARE TIMES in our life when we must laugh about the things we used to do before we came to know the Lord. At first, when we accepted Jesus as Lord and Savior of our life, we were on fire for the Word of God. The Word of God truly had transforming power, and we found that we couldn't get enough of God's Word. It was like going into a room that was always dark and then one day we went in the room and there was light. It was a light brighter than any light I've ever seen. God's love lit our way, warmed our soul, and chipped away at all the hard places in our heart. God's love gave us a whole new attitude. Now, we began to see our life and the world through the eyes of God, and everything took on new meaning. We were in a better place mentally, emotionally, and spiritually. We were on a new path. God changed our trajectory.

By now, you already know that God made some big changes in our lives. We loved God and loved our new life. Unfortunately, as with all things, nothing ever stays the same. Although we would love for some things to never change, life doesn't work like that. Life is always changing because that is how God designed things. We, of course, are subject to the world we live in, but we are foreigners in a land that is not our home. We are visitors staying for a while until it is time for us to move on to a heavenly home that God has so promised us. In the meantime, while we are here, God has assigned each of us to a good work. He has not placed us here to sit around and watch life go by.

The Merriam-Webster Dictionary defines "assignment" as a "specified task or amount of work assigned or undertaken as if assigned by authority." In this sense, the person of authority is our Father in Heaven. In 1 Corinthians 7:17 (NLT), the Apostle Paul says, "Each of you should continue to live in whatever situation the Lord has placed you and remain as you were when God first called you. This is my rule for all the churches." You see, we do not get to choose the assignment, but we do get to choose to partner with God to carry out His work. We are empowered by our assignment and rewarded according to our labor for the Lord.

A few years passed from what I classify as our Damascus Road experience. We were doing as so many couples, trying to navigate through the maze of marriage and seeing what it means to do Proverbs 3:5 (KJV), "trust in the Lord and lean not to your own understanding." Little did we know that God was revealing the next steps in our new trajectory. David was called into ministry and a few years later, so was I. Now when David informed me of this clarion call that he believed he had received from God, I was truly floored. Why on earth would God call this guy when we were just getting our act together? Was this a joke? Was God really calling this guy to ministry? This was the man who struggled with drugs and alcohol. This was the man who would leave home going to the store and return a few hours later higher than a kite. God, are you calling the one who had mommy and daddy issues? How on earth could he minister to others when he was just finding himself? Yes, God had jokes. I could think of a million things we could do, and ministry was not one of them. A few years later, God called me to ministry as well. Unlike David, I surrendered to the call of God after a great deal of kicking and screaming. Once again, I asked God, "Where on earth do you get these ideas? You called us both to ministry?" I got over the fact that He called David, but to add me to the plan was not what I had in mind. I did not see how God could use someone like me to minister to others when I suffered from low self-esteem, malicious parent syndrome, emotional abuse, and a host of other issues. I never believed that anything I did was ever good enough. So, I thought God called folks who had their act together? I certainly did not think God utilized people who struggled each day to stay focused on the most important things in life. I asked God many times how in the world could I help anyone else? You see, it is those kind of people God looks for to do the work of ministry. God is not looking for those who have it all together and who have dotted every "I" in their lives and crossed every "T." He is looking for the ones like David and I who must take one day at a time. God is looking for the people who can reflect the light of Jesus and the love He shared with us to others.

Answering the call of God was scary to say the least. I reflected on how Moses reacted to his calling from God. If you recall, Moses was a Hebrew boy raised in the house of the Pharoah of Egypt. As a young man, Moses killed an Egyptian whom he found beating another Hebrew. He fled to the land of Midian and became a shepherd. It was in that land that God called Moses to ministry. Moses was like many of us who cannot see what God sees in us. We cannot imagine that God could use those who have so many failures and never saw themselves as being worthy to carry out something so important. How was God going use a couple who had so many issues? How was God going to use people who just started walking the path of salvation themselves? Crazy as it seems, God called a murderer named Moses to lead his people out of slavery. In Exodus 3:11–12 (NIV), the Word of God says, "But Moses said to God, 'Who am I that I should go to Pharaoh, and that I should bring the children of Israel out of Egypt?' So He said, 'I will certainly be with you. And this shall be a sign to you that I have sent you: When you have brought the people out of Egypt, you shall serve God on this mountain." You see, when God calls us, He equips us. We need to have a heart and a mind to serve. Moses struggled with his call from God because he began to see obstacles and make excuses. We see the following exchange between Moses and God in Exodus 4:1-5 (NLT),

> "Then Moses answered and said, 'But suppose they will not believe me or listen to my voice; suppose they say, "The LORD has not appeared to you."' So the LORD said to him, 'What is that in your hand?' He said, 'A rod.' And He said, 'Cast it on the ground.' So, he cast it on the ground, and it became a serpent; and Moses fled from it. Then the LORD said to Moses, 'Reach out your hand and take it by the tail' (and he reached out his hand and caught it,

and it became a rod in his hand), 'that
they may believe that the LORD God
of their fathers, the God of Abraham,
the God of Isaac, and the God of Jacob,
has appeared to you (Exodus 4:1-5).'"

Moses did exactly what many of us do, give excuses
for why we feel we cannot do what God called us to do.
What we fail to realize is that our call from God is not
because we are qualified or we have many skills, it is
because we are vessels for his use. God provides everything we need. Just as Moses doubted his ability, God
saw the better part and provided everything he would
need to carry out the call. As Moses did, we also had
every excuse in the book as to why we were not the best
choice for ministry. Our calls were not only to minister
the Word of God to people but also to minister to married couples who had abandoned ship and given up any
hope to save their marriages. God called us to the one
thing we believed was our greatest area of failure—marriage. Yes, God had jokes. He called us to use His Word,
our history, and our experience to share with other married couples. Wow, what a mandate. Who would have
thought that two broken people who came out of dysfunctional histories could help others? Well, with God
all things are possible.

Out of our call, a marriage ministry was birth. In
His Will Marriage Ministry Inc. God choreographed

our steps into a ministry to help married couples. The mission of In His Will Marriage Ministry was to educate and enlighten couples with relationship fundamentals that could assist in nurturing a strong and eternal godly love. Our ministry first began by being invited to speak as a couple at a Valentine's Day gathering. Saying that we were clueless as to what we would say was an understatement. We had no idea what we could possibly say that would be of any value. But just as we offered our last excuses, God reminded us that if He called us, He qualified us, and He equipped us. In the fourth chapter of Exodus, Moses was also fearful that he was not a good speaker and that he would not be able to carry out this assignment from God. Exodus 4:10–17 (NLT) reads:

> But Moses pleaded with the LORD, "O Lord, I'm not very good with words. I never have been, and I'm not now, even though you have spoken to me. I get tongue-tied, and my words get tangled." Then the LORD asked Moses, "Who makes a person's mouth? Who decides whether people speak or do not speak, hear or do not hear, see or do not see? Is it not I, the LORD? Now go! I will be with you as you speak, and I will instruct you in what to say." But Moses again

pleaded, "Lord, please! Send anyone else." Then the LORD became angry with Moses. "All right," he said. "What about your brother, Aaron the Levite? I know he speaks well. And look! He is on his way to meet you now. He will be delighted to see you. Talk to him and put the words in his mouth. I will be with both of you as you speak, and I will instruct you both in what to do. Aaron will be your spokesman to the people. He will be your mouthpiece, and you will stand in the place of God for him, telling him what to say. And take your shepherd's staff with you and use it to perform the miraculous signs I have shown you (Exodus 4:10-17)."

There are no excuses you can give God when He sets you on your new trajectory. He knows all, and He sees all. He has already anticipated what you are going to say, what you are going to do and when you are going to do it. This is the God who created our end before our beginning. He is the sovereign and all-sufficient God. Adequate to accomplish every purpose and to meet every need. God created the world out of nothing, which meant he could make a wonderful something out of us. Yes, God had jokes. God's joke was calling us to ministry. The last laugh was on us believing the lies of the enemy that we could not be of any use to an all mighty, loving, and sovereign God who can do anything but fail.

Chapter Eight

It Is Time to Forgive

"For if you forgive other people when they sin against You, your heavenly Father will also forgive you."— Matthew 6:14 (NIV)

THE IMPORTANCE OF forgiveness in a marriage can never be understated. Forgiving our spouses for offenses or sins they committed against us can become an overwhelming challenge. Our hearts must be pliable, so that God can soften the hard places that have developed due to pain and hurt. Our marriages can become stifled because of the harm that unforgiveness plants. Often, as human beings we find great difficulty in admitting our faults or any offense we may have committed. In fact, many find it very difficult to even utter the words, "I'm sorry." In the beginning of our marriage, the words "I'm sorry" were extremely difficult for me and David.

We couldn't bring ourselves to say those two small words because to each of us those words meant we were admitting that we did something wrong. Those two small words alone represented a surrender by one of us, which was not happening. When we learned to cultivate a heart of repentance in our marriage, we learned how to keep the enemy at bay. The devil's goal was to navigate a way into to our marriage and wreak havoc until we both threw up our hands and the marriage would be over. By cultivating a heart of forgiveness, we learned how to allow the power of the Holy Spirit to come in and heal our wounded hearts.

Forgiveness helped us remove the roadblocks we had allowed to come into our marriage. Forgiving one another also reflected our respect for each other and our respect for God. Because forgiveness was a part of God's divine plan, it positioned us to be obedient to His will. In Ephesians 4:32 (NIV) the Word of God, states, "And be kind to one another, tenderhearted, forgiving one another, even as God in Christ forgave you." So, God stood by ready and willing to forgive us for our sins, but He asked that we extend the same forgiveness to each other first. The Apostle Paul expressed how we should seek to show the same kindness, tender heartedness, and forgiveness to others that God showed to us. If we treat others as God treats us, we fulfill everything that the Apostle Paul expressed for us to do. Our forgiveness of our spouses must be patterned after the forgiveness that God taught in His Word. When we think of the amazing way God forgave us, it is terrible for us to withhold forgiveness from those who have wronged us.

I must say that when David's life began to change for the better, I had a hard time believing him. I will never forget when he came home after the T.D. Jakes conference and proclaimed, "Jesus has pleaded my case." I did not know what he meant by that statement but either way, he was going to need more than a statement about Jesus pleading his case. I looked for evidence for some real change. If you recall, after the Lord set me straight on the things I needed to work on, I found myself less preoccupied with how David was going to be changed. If Jesus truly was pleading his case, sooner or later things would begin to change. The truth be told, change had to start with me. I needed to forgive this man the same way God had forgiven me. I needed to allow David an opportunity to allow God to do great work in him and great work in me. We first had to begin with those words that were so hard to utter, "I am sorry; will you forgive me?" You would have thought someone killed us every time we tried to utter those words. You see, that's right where the enemy wanted us to be stuck. Satan wanted us to hold on to hurt and pain. He wanted us to replay the myriad of episodes in our mind that caused us to stall out and not ask for forgiveness. It's not enough for us to go to God and lament and ask for forgiveness, we must go to the person we have committed the offense against. We must utter the words "I am sorry for all that I have done to you, and I ask you to forgive me as God desires." Once we stepped across the threshold of forgiveness, it was like a giant weight was lifted off our shoulders. We had taken the first step. First, we asked God to forgive us because in His Word He says that if we confess our sins, He is faithful and just to forgive us and cleanse us from all unrighteousness. Then, we forgave each other. What a breath of freedom to experience and know that our Father in Heaven has seen fit to forgive us for the myriad of things we have done and still do. He sent Jesus here to this earth to complete a great work. Hebrews 4:16 (NKJV) says, "Let us therefore come boldly to the throne of grace, that we may obtain mercy and find grace to help in time of need." We were finally free from the bondages of sin. Our past no longer belonged to us because the Son of God had set us free.

Forgiveness, just like salvation, is a process. The first step is to take a plunge and ask to be forgiven. Forgiveness begins with the spouse first asking to be forgiven and then making the apology. There must be a willingness on the part of both parties to forgive and make amends for what has taken place. Then comes the big step, having the patience to see the process through. There must be patience for the one forgiving and patience for the one who needs forgiveness. Finally, there must be a commitment to rebuild the trust that was either badly damaged or lost. We must be able to let go of the past and the things that have happened and begin the process of building a new future. We must learn from our past mistakes to never repeat again. Our objective is to not allow our past to hold us hostage in the future.

The biggest challenge in dealing with a lack of forgiveness in a marriage is earning back the trust we lost. The Merriam-Webster Dictionary defines "trust" as "assured reliance on the character, ability, strength, or truth of someone or something." In other words, I can count on you if I cannot count on anything else. Trust is built over time in relationships. The same trust that we have when we sit down in a chair is the trust we have, or should have, in our marital relationships. The average person never questions whether a chair will hold them, but they do not spend time developing confidence that the chair is sturdy. In most cases, even if we enter a room for the first time, we do not question whether the chair will break from under us as soon as we are seated.

Marital trust develops over time through experiences together. The investment in each other builds a sturdy platform on which to rely on one another. We feel about our relationship, or at least, we should feel about our relationship, just like we feel about the chair. I can count on you to not let me down, or in the case of the chair, I can count on the chair to not break out from under me. Once trust is violated, whether it is from marital infidelity, financial issues or failures, lack of honesty or truthfulness, the bridge to trust can be very difficult to mend. Many times, one spouse wants to be forgiven and pick up where they left off before things became unhinged and act as if the incident or issue never happen. Unfortunately, losing one's trust is never that simple to repair. It took time to bend, break, and destroy the level of trust David and I had in our relationship. So, it was going to take time to piece together the broken pieces of this marriage. Mending marital fences takes time and effort. Marriages don't get repaired overnight. It is only in movies that the couple comes back together, makes love, and the next day, all is forgiven. It takes intervention from our heavenly Father, two yielded vessels ready to be placed back on the potter's wheel, and a lot of patience. Yes, patience, my friend, truly must have its perfect work. With God, all things are possible. With time and work, God can get you back on the right track if both heart's desire for that to happen. No one wants to pay for past mistakes for the rest of their lives, but you must do it God's way. It can't be a halfhearted attempt at forgiveness and reconciliation. You see, one thing about God, once true repentance takes place, He does not need us to continue repeatedly paying for our failures. In the sight of God, repentance is a complete change of direction. We turn away from those things that we have done wrong, never to do them again. Romans 5:8 (NKJV) states, "God demonstrates His own love toward us, in that while we were still sinners, Christ died for us." Imagine that. God loved us in our mess. So, how dare we withhold forgiveness from our spouses. I know by now you are asking, "What if he or she cheated on me?" I'm saying forgive. "What if they left me and the children?" I'm saying forgive. "What if they used me and took all my money?" I'm saying forgive. Forgiveness helps us to move on with our lives. Forgiveness causes us to line up with the will of God for our lives. Now, does that mean you are going to continue the marriage? I can't say, but it does mean that you have begun the steps to become whole again. You can be free and not held hostage to your past. Where you go from there must be an individual choice. David and I both chose to forgive each other and allow God to build a brand-new foundation underneath. This time, it would be stronger and as the commercial says, it would be "Ford Tough" or better yet, "God Tough."

Chapter Nine

Two are Better than One

"Two are better than one, Because they have a good reward for their labor. For if they fall, one will lift up his companion. But woe to him who is alone when he falls, For he has no one to help him up. Again, if two lie down together, they will keep warm; But how can one be warm alone? Though one may be overpowered by another, two can withstand him. And a threefold cord is not quickly broken. — Ecclesiastes 4:9–13 (NKJV)

God created marriage to fulfill companionship and relationship. Marriage began in the Garden of Eden with Adam and Eve where God began His ultimate design for creation. His purpose for marriage was to provide partnership, spiritual intimacy, and the ability to pursue God together with your mate. Marriages were created to mirror God's covenant relationship with His people. In 1 Corinthians 13:4-8 (NKJV) the scripture states;

> [4] Love suffers long *and* is kind; love does not envy; love does not parade itself, is not puffed up; [5] does not behave rudely, does not seek its own, is not provoked, thinks no evil; [6] does not rejoice in iniquity, but rejoices in the truth; [7] bears all things, believes all things, hopes all things, endures all things. [8] Love never fails. But whether *there are* prophecies, they will fail; whether *there are* tongues, they will cease; whether *there is* knowledge, it will vanish away.

God created the marriage to demonstrate His love. God loved us so much that He wanted to provide the world with a picture of His love for mankind. God gave man the gift of uniting a man and a woman, whose relationship, would reflect the loving relationship between Christ and His church. God created the husband to be the leader in the home to love and serve his wife as Christ loves the church. The wife is to respect and submit to her husband as she respects and submits to Christ. We demonstrate our love for God through our marriages, and marriages make it when we learn to live by God's principles and His plans. God calls both man and woman to submit their lives to Him and to one another, as a sign of the covenant bond that He desires to have with them. So, if we can trust God to take care of our eternities, we can certainly trust God to take care of our marriages.

In Ecclesiastes (NIV), King Solomon reflected on the importance of companionship and the benefits of people working together. In Ecclesiastes 4:9 (NKJV), Solomon said, "Two are better than one, because they have a good return for their labor." He agreed with God in Genesis 2:18 (NIV), which states, "It is not good for the man to be alone." Solomon continued in Ecclesiastes 4:10 (NKJV), "If they fall, one will lift up his companion. But woe to him who is alone when he falls, for he has no one to help him up." The idea here is that when two people are married, if they work together, they can help each other out during challenging and difficult times. They can also reap great benefits working together in good times. Couples working together can become productive and fruitful, which glorifies God. In Ecclesiastes 4:12 (NKJV), Solomon said, "Though one may be overpowered by another, two can withstand him. And a threefold cord is not quickly broken." Solomon emphasized the idea that companionship was a good thing, and a third cord illustrated that a relationship intertwined with God was a three-fold cord that could not be easily broken. Simply put, if God is in the midst, the opportunity for success is far greater.

During the early years of our marriage, I didn't quite fathom how two was better than one. In fact, what I tended to fall to most of the time was the old saying, "I can do bad all by myself." If things are not going well in your relationship, it's very easy to feel that it's not worth the effort to stay in a relationship and be miserable. You begin to feel that being by yourself doing bad is more palatable than having a companion and you are still doing just as bad or worse. I felt my situation, or should I say my marriage, at the time was bad. I felt I was bad, David was bad, everything around us was bad. Our children were the only bright spots in our marriage. As I mentioned earlier, we had a lot of help with them. God always knows how to insert the right people in your life to keep you from totally making a mess, and that includes making a mess of your children. When God is righting the ship, He won't allow you to do anything that will interfere with His plan or purpose. Nevertheless, David and I didn't see the perfect plan that God lined up for us. I couldn't see us working together and I certainly didn't see a third cord (God) in our relationship. As I think back now, perhaps if we had taken the time to sit down and listen to each other for a few minutes, we might have stumbled upon some ways we could work together. How do you listen when both people are talking? Unfortunately, challenging marriages don't generally allow for listening. Perhaps, if we had someone in our lives at the time who could have given us marital counseling, we could have done better. When David and I got married, marriage counselors were not talked about as much as they are now. Back in the day, couples in our circle didn't do a lot of talking about marriage counseling or anything related to marriage enrichment. In most cases, the advice of the day was to stay in your marriage or just get a boyfriend or girlfriend on the side. I can say that the idea of going with someone else while I was married didn't have much appeal. I don't know about David, but if I could not handle one man, what in the world was I going to do with two? A secret lover and a husband were too much trouble to me, and I was too miserable at the time for anything extra in my life.

Challenging marriages only allow for fussing, fighting, arguing, cursing, and now and then a broken dish or two. Just as a side note, I was one of those women who, if I couldn't seem to get my point across, would throw dishes, lamps, books—you name it. If it could fly, it was fair game. David was good at staying a fair distance away to prevent being in the line of fire. Working together was not something we were good at. We either didn't know how to work together or we didn't want to work together. You see, the beauty of working with God is that all things have a way of working to your good. Romans 8:38 (KJV) states, "And we know that all things work together for good to them that love God, to them who are the called according to his purpose." David Guzik, in his Enduring Word Commentary explained:

> God's sovereignty and ability to manage every aspect of our lives is demonstrated in the fact that all things work together for good to those who love God. He can make even those sufferings work together for our good and his good. God can work all things, not some things and He works them for good together, not in isolation. This promise is for those who love God in the Biblical understanding of love, and it expresses that God manages the affairs of our life because we are called according to His purpose (Romans 8:38, Enduring Word Commentary).

Two of the hallmarks of a thriving marriage are learning and understanding the plan of God for marriages. David and I had the best intentions, but we were ignorant of the things of God. We didn't know that God had a plan for us, and it did not include us getting a divorce. We did not understand that the plan God had for us originated back at the Garden of Eden when He put Adam to sleep, and He created Eve from one of his ribs. Genesis 2:18 (NIV) states, "The LORD God said, 'It is not good that man should be alone; I will make him a helper comparable to him.'" So, right then and there He created Eve. Genesis 2:22 (NKJV) states, "Then the rib which the Lord God had taken from man He made into a woman, and He brought her to the man. And Adam said: 'This is now bone of my bones And flesh of my flesh; She shall be called Woman, Because she was taken out of Man.'" It is right there in the garden that God gave Adam and Eve their first assignment—their purpose. Genesis 1:28 (NKJV) says, "Then God blessed them, and God said to them, "Be fruitful and multiply; fill the earth and subdue it; have dominion over the fish of the sea, over the birds of the air, and over every living thing that moves on the earth." Adam and Eve were to become one flesh by working together and being inter-twined with God. They were to come together and have children, raise a family, and run the earth. That is what God desires for us as married couples. He desires us to work together with Him.

In the later years, as David and I began to dig into the Word of God, we saw God's purpose and plan for our lives, marriage, and family. We didn't realize that it was not just about David and me, but it was about our children. It was about their future. It was about ending once and for all the generational curse of separation and divorce in our families. It was about ending the alcohol and drug abuse. It was about ending the physical and emotional abuse that had flowed through generations in our families. It was about the love of God covering a multitude of sins. What example were we setting for our children? What kind of lives were we teaching our children that they should live? One thing I love about God is that He will not let you mess up His plans for you. Now, you may have to take the wilderness route, which will probably take you a little longer to get where you need to be, but you can count on God to see it through.

We yielded our lives to God and allowed Him to mold and shape us into the parents we needed to be, not the ones we wanted to be but what we needed to be for our children. They needed to know that just because you start out wrong doesn't mean that God can't get you back on track. It is better to have two instead of one. As David and I continued to grow in the things of God, we became closer. We learned how to submit to God and how to submit to each other. We gave our children real parents who invested in their lives. David showed me, and our children what happens when the man gets in place and his steps are ordered by the Lord. We could see how working together could have great benefits. We relied on each other and supported each other through the challenges that came later. We saw how we could get so much more done, not numerically, but spiritually, emotionally, and mentally. God revealed to us how the covenant plan He established was supposed to work, and the benefit of a better and whole life. The story of

Jonathan and David is an excellent example of the covenant relationship that God desires for us. Their covenant was an agreement that could not be easily broken. A covenant means that you don't harm each other; you protect each other. It means I've got your back, and you have my back no matter what happens. That's why two is so much better than one. When you are in covenant with someone, you are joined together and identified with each other. No matter what comes, you have what you need. As David and I began to line up with the plans of God, things began to fall in place. God downloaded His plan for our lives in us, and He laid out a marital plan of respect, support, esteem, love, and laughter. The best part, I wasn't going to be alone. I was going to have the one person by my side who had stuck it out with me all the way.

CHAPTER TEN

TRANSFORMED BY GOD'S GRACE

> "But by the grace of God I am what I am, and His grace toward me was not in vain; but I labored more abundantly than they all, yet not I, but the grace of God which was with me." — 1 Corinthians 15:10 (NKJV)

EPHESIANS 2:8–9, (NKJV) states, "For by grace you have been saved through faith, and that not of yourselves; it is the gift of God, 9 not of works, lest anyone should boast."

When someone or something is "transformed," the Merriam-Webster dictionary says that it means "that there is a thorough or dramatic change in the form, appearance, or character." Just as the butterfly goes through four stages of metamorphosis, we go through the stages of change, when God is transforming us. It has nothing to do with our outward appearance. It's great to improve your looks or work toward self-improvement, but God changes us from the inside out. 2 Corinthians 3:18 (NKJV) states, "But we all, with unveiled face, beholding as in a mirror the glory of the Lord, are being transformed into the same image from glory to glory, just as by the Spirit of the Lord." Our change manifests in stages and it begins with an encounter with God.

It is amazing how we think our life change should be an explosion or an epic event—fireworks, and all. You see, God doesn't have to create an explosive event to have a first encounter with us. We can see in the Bible an excellent example of how God can engage us with a still, small voice. In 1 Kings 19:9–13, the Prophet Elijah ran from Jezebel and ended up at Mt. Sinai, better known as the "Mountain of God." The Lord spoke to Elijah and asked him why he was there on the mountain. In 1 Kings 19:11 (KJV), Elijah was told to go out and stand before the Lord on the mountain. As he waited, the Scripture states that Elijah sought the Lord in a mighty windstorm which hit the mountain, but the Lord was not there. Then, there was an earthquake and a fire, but God was not in those either. God came and spoke in a gentle whisper. All that Elijah imagined God would show up in, He didn't. That's how God begins our process of transformation. It is that still, small voice of the Holy Spirit that begins to draw us in. Our introduction to God can start as an annoying co-worker telling you about God or a nosey relative sowing seeds of God's Word in your life. It can even be a T.D. Jakes conference that you attend, where Jesus pleads your case. Now don't get me wrong, some of us may need an epic event to draw us in, but I believe David and I were just like Elijah. We expected God in the thunder, and He knew we needed His whisper. God put in the fix just like they do in a fight. The outcome was going to be a win. We just didn't know it. Little by little, God took us through the stages of transformation. Whether we believed it or not, God knew us long before we were in our mother's womb (Jeremiah 1:5, KJV). He already knew our end from our beginning. He knew where and when our lives were to begin the metamorphosis. I laugh at how we can think that following God was some great idea we came up with on our own and just like that, we started following Him. It is true that we have a choice, but God chose us first. God drew us out of the jungle of destruction at an appointed time and set us on a new path. God caused us to shed old skin and start taking on new skin—or better yet—a new way of life.

Of course, there are those who would ask David and I if staying married was worth it. I would say at this moment and time that it was well worth it. David and I came to a crossroads where we had to decide, how far were we willing to go to save our marriage. What we didn't know was that it was not about saving our marriage it was about surrendering our will and lives to God's will and allowing Him to form the marriage that He desired for His plan to be fulfilled. David was never going to be the man I wanted, and I wasn't going to be the woman he wanted. We had to be the man and woman that God wanted. Strangely enough, I must say that we both got the best deal. We got each other, and we got God. We got a three-fold cord that could not be easily broken. David and I decided that our marriage was worth saving. We had children, and we didn't want them to join the statistics of children from divorced parents. We didn't want our children trying to please both parents and never realizing that if a person is not happy with themselves, they certainly can't be happy with you. We wanted our children to know what a family healed and whole looked like. The only way we were going to get that was to surrender our lives to God and allow Him to do the work in us. I can tell you that it was not easy. Many times, I know I wanted to throw up my hands and walk out, but God was always there with a still, small voice giving me the nudge I needed when I got frustrated or disappointed. I know, God was with David. I could see him being molded and shaped into the man I never imagined. He became a man of integrity and honor. He became confident in who he was and who he belonged to, and most of all he became a man after God's own heart. I began to see more of God in David each day as time moved forward. I could trust

God more and more for the man David became and the woman that I was becoming. It was wonderful to look in the mirror years down the road and, to my excitement, I didn't see the person I saw so long ago. What I saw was what God saw, someone who was fearfully and wonderfully made (Psalm 139:14, KJV). I finally saw the Proverbs 31 woman I always read about in the Bible. I can't tell you that I was not afraid many times. I would have anxiety every time David walked out the door to go to the store or anywhere because I just knew he either would not come back, or he would come back like he used to come back. I was often reminded by the scripture in Proverbs 3:5–6 (NKJV), which states, "Trust in the Lord with all your heart and lean not on your own understanding; In all your ways acknowledge Him, And He shall direct your paths." Faced with what you see, sometimes it is so hard to trust God and lean not to your own understanding. Your senses show you one thing, which is in stark contrast to what God wants you to see. Little by little, those senses begin to draw you away from trusting God. It is so important that we see every situation through the eyes of God, or we will collapse.

Remember, at the beginning of my story, I told you that you can have a grand wedding, but if the foundation of your marriage is weak and fragile, the gloriousness of the wedding will not mean a thing. Yes, it will be a beautiful wedding with all the trimmings, but that's all it will be because you didn't involve the great wedding planner. David and I had no idea of how to build a strong marriage. Like many people, we assumed we would figure it out as we went along. There are no self-help books or research studies out there that can truly show you the way. You can Google a lot of stuff and you can watch a lot of the newest television programs where people pride themselves in being experts in the field of marital bliss. You can go to marriage therapists, pastors, family members, and anyone else, but until you decide that you are ready to put the time and the work in, you are wasting time. One size doesn't fit all, and you and your spouse must make a commitment to do the work. Besides, every marriage is different, and each marriage has its own blueprint that God laid out specifically for those in that marriage. Each marriage must have the common thread of the Holy Spirit. There can be no substitute for the right instructions to guide you through the process.

Marriage is like building a house. Proverbs 14:1 (KJV) states, "Every wise woman buildeth her house: but the foolish plucketh it down with her hands." In this passage of Scripture, Solomon was describing how a wise woman is concerned about her family. She blesses her family by ensuring their needs are met and she is eager to live out the call that God has on her life. The foolish woman is not concerned with the needs of the children or the husband. Everything is centered around her, and her efforts do more to damage the family than to build them up. The foolish woman is unknowledgeable or unskilled. When you don't have the skill or the knowledge to do what is required to build a marriage then you can only tear down what God has put in place. Proverbs 19:14, (KJV) states, "Unless the Lord builds a house, the house is built in vain." When a house is constructed, the house must be built on a solid foundation. If the foundation is not solid, then the house will fall. When houses are constructed, many components must come together for a builder to lay down a foundation that is strong. The builder must ensure that the foundation meets all the necessary requirements before the house can be built. The builder helps you create the right blueprints for your home (marriage). Once the blueprint is created, the building of the house begins. Building codes and guidelines enable the builder to ensure that the foundation they are creating will withstand whatever may come against the building throughout time. The Word of God is our building code for marriages. God has already laid out the specific codes and guidelines in His scriptures for us to build the foundation of marriage. If God doesn't build the house, then the house is built in vain. Remember, the ultimate builder of a marriage is God himself and there is no substitute.

In the Sermon on the Mount, Jesus taught the disciples a multitude of truths. One of those truths was about building a house on a firm foundation so that when the storms of life came, the house would stand. Jesus explained how important it was to hear the Word and to do the Word during His Sermon on the Mount. In Matthew 7:24–27, (KJV), He said,

> Therefore, whosoever heareth these sayings of mine, and doeth them, I will liken him unto a wise man, which built his house upon a rock: And the rain descended, and the floods came, and the winds blew, and beat upon that house; and it fell not: for it was founded upon a rock. And everyone that heareth these sayings of mine, and doeth them not, shall be likened unto a foolish man, which built his house on the sand: And the rain descended, and the floods came, and the winds blew, and beat upon that house; and it fell: and great was the fall of it (Matthew 7:24-27).

Jesus told the people there was nothing that could be substituted for a firm foundation. When the storms of life come barreling against a home that has a firm foundation, it will be just as He described it—the house will be strong and sturdy, and it will not fall. That is why we must be connected to God. In Proverbs 19:14 (NIV), the Word of God states, "Houses and riches are the inheritance from the fathers, but a prudent wife is from the Lord." A prudent wife is intelligent and skillful because it takes skill and intelligence to build a home. Now don't get all in your feelings. I'm not suggesting that you must be a Harvard Law student to build your marriage, but you do have to have the skill, knowledge, and intelligence that comes directly from God. The skill, knowledge, and intelligence of the world will only cause you to embrace concepts that the world system supports. Those concepts are faulty, and one size must fit all. Couples need more than a television counselor to advise them on marriage. The world system doesn't really care if marriages survive or not. But God cares. It takes God's wisdom and knowledge to build a strong marriage. It's all about His plan and His process. Everyone has levels and stages they go through in their marriages. If you don't know or fear God, then you are incapable of wisely building a strong marriage.

I had to learn over time that it truly takes a wise woman to build her home. It must be a woman who has the faith, trust, and relationship with God to become wise. Becoming a wise woman is a process. I would love to tell you that it comes overnight, but it doesn't. Wisdom must come through trial and error, but the growth process must be guided by God's Word. Proverbs 2:6 (NIV) states, "For the LORD gives wisdom; From His mouth come knowledge and understanding." James 1:5, (NLT) states, "If you need wisdom, ask our generous God, and

he will give it to you. He will not rebuke you for asking."
So, when we enter a relationship with God, through
faith, godly wisdom is made available to us. Our willingness to seek God for His wisdom will enable us to
be shielded from evil and cause our journey to be well.
God's truth and knowledge can guide us through the
pitfalls of marriage. We can be confident if we trust
Him and lean not to our own understanding that He
will direct our path.

We are now at forty-three years of marriage. I certainly never thought we would get this far, but we did.
I look over at David sometimes, and I am so glad I did
not throw in the towel. In fact, I'm glad he did not throw
in the towel either. I believe that our being together was
meant to be. There are far more things I could have
added in this writing about our marriage, but how many
ways can you say, "Trust God?" How many ways can
you describe how God's grace swept in and made the
crooked things straight, and the rough places smooth?
There are many more things I could have written about
our lives, and the numerous mountains that we had to
climb. Don't get me wrong, many joys were sprinkled
in with our trials and challenges. But God made sure
that He didn't let go of us and we clearly didn't let go
of Him. Only through God's grace can I say we sur-
vived all the things we experienced. More importantly,
God became the captain of my ship and the head of my
life. He became the commander and chief of our lives.

We allowed God to show us unimaginable things. God didn't just save us, He changed us.

So how are things going now after all these years? Things are going great. We enjoy every second, every moment, every hour, and every day of our lives. God gave us double for our trouble. We have been married going on forty-four years. For all the years that were filled with turbulence, we have enjoyed double the number of years of joy. Now, we still are learning and growing more and more each day. This is not a bus stop situation. God doesn't just drop you off after you have gone through His training program. God's training is for life. We are still being molded and shaped into His image. Are there occasional bumps in the road? Of course, there are. It wouldn't be life if we didn't have bumps in the road. We wouldn't need God if we didn't have those. Now, we can speak to our mountains in authority, and it will be moved, and we can do as Job 22:28 (KJV) tells us, "Thou shalt also decree a thing, and it shall be established unto thee: and the light shall shine upon thy ways." God continues to give us the tools as we continue to trust in Him and lean not to our own understanding. He provides a way of escape every single time; and yes, there are tests. Unfortunately, there are times we flunk the test, but because of God's grace, we can take the test again and get it right. God is a God of second and third chances. On a personal note, I would probably do some serious consultation with God if I kept having to take the same test over and over. Repeatedly failing the same test means more study is needed. That's just a word to the wise.

I now desire to be the best wife I can be for God and for David. I believe the same is true for David. Our children are out and about living their best lives. What I know now would have probably saved me a tremendous amount of heartache and headache years ago. You know, we like to look back and ask the question, "If I could do this over again, would I do it differently?" The answer to that question would be a resounding "No." This journey was for us, and this was the way we had to go. It was to teach, train, and equip us for service in the kingdom. There are couples out there who are hanging onto the edge of despair, and they need to know that if they surrender to God, they can make it through. Somebody must be able to show them a testimony of what it looks like to get to the other side. It won't be pretty, and it won't be easy, but it will be worth it. No matter what, you win in the end because God causes us to be triumphant. Knowing God must be a lifestyle. Today I can truly say, "What the enemy meant for bad, God turned it to our good." God transformed us with His amazing grace, and He took two very dysfunctional people and made them functional for the kingdom. You see, 1 Corinthians 1:27 (KJV) states, "But God hath chosen the foolish things of the world to confound the wise; and God hath chosen the weak things of the world to confound the things which are mighty." God chose to transform us, not because we were so great, but because he is so great God. God used two very imperfect people to serve in his kingdom. The world's wisdom and ways will not bring us to salvation. God does not call us because we are educated or profound, He calls us because His way of salvation is foolish to those of the world, and it is only through our faith in Jesus Christ that we can be saved.

A healthy marriage helps others to see our God and his love for us. I am so glad He chose us and guided us along the way. Our reality is that our journey is not over, it is just beginning. There is more work to be done in the kingdom and more transformation to take place in us and in you. I encourage you to let the transformation happen and wait with joyous expectation for what God has in store for you in the future. I can't wait to see what God has in store for us.

References

BibleGateway. "BibleGateway.com: A Searchable Online Bible in over 150 Versions and 50 Languages." *Biblegateway.com*, BibleGateway, 1993, www.biblegateway.com/.

"Romans Chapter 8." *Enduring Word*, 17 Dec. 2015, enduringword.com/bible-commentary/romans-8/38. Accessed 12 Feb. 2022.

"Money Ruining Marriages in America: A Ramsey Solutions study", Feb 7, 2018, https://www.daveramsey.com/pr/money-ruining-marriages-in-america.

"G5293 - Hypotassō - Strong's Greek Lexicon (Kjv)." *Blue Letter Bible*, www.blueletterbible.org/lexicon/g5293/kjv/tr/0-1/.

ABOUT THE AUTHORS

Elders David and Jessica Swain reside in Madison, Georgia, and they have been married for forty-three years. David is employed in Milledgeville, Georgia, as a composite-tooler and Jessica is a retiree from  Georgia College and State University of Milledgeville, Georgia. The Swains have two children, Dr. JaBaris Swain and Mrs. Kristen Wilson. Kristen and her husband, Jamar, have two children, Alexis Kennedy, and Zion David. The Swains are members of Abundant Life Word Fellowship in Eatonton, Georgia, under the Pastoral leadership of Dr. George and Enobong Utuk.

Their ministry, In His Will Marriage Ministry, Inc., seeks to educate, and enlighten both couples and singles with relationship fundamentals that could assist in nurturing a strong and eternal, godly love. The vision of In His Will Marriage Ministry is to help couples understand the covenant relationship of marriage, the benefits that God has provided, and how to victoriously walk in marriage.